The No. 2 Parenting Book:

PRACTICAL TIPS FOR THE POOPED OUT PARENT

Andrea D. Mata, Ph.D.

The identities of most people in this book have been altered.

Copyright @2023 Andrea Mata

All rights reserved. No part of this book may be reproduced in any manner without the prior written permission of the copyright owner.

Editor: Nicole Diederich, Ph.D.
Cover design: Lauren Marshall
Illustrations: Adam Lauritsen
Page layout: Anne Beekman

ISBN# 979-8-89298-683-0

Table of Contents

Introduction 3

The Fundamentals

All Is Not Lost.. 9

You Can't Parent from the Couch 13

Consistency, Consistency, Consistency...................... 19

Adapt!.. 25

One Size Doesn't Fit All 33

Give Them Just Enough 37

Sentencing Your Child to a Life in Your Basement....... 43

Stop the Busyness 51

High Expectations

Taming Temper Tantrums 59

Why Kids Do What They Do 67

Seeing Red 73

Cool as a Cucumber 81

Catch and Ignore.. 89

Positive Reinforcement, Your First Line of Defense 95

Treat Your Child's Behavior Like Play-Doh 101

Tell. Don't Ask. 107

Five Second Rule 113

Hand Over Hand 119

Your Child, The Escape Artist 125

The 4 R's of Logical Consequences 131

Tired of Nagging? Use Natural Consequences 139

The Warm and Fuzzies

Your Ratio's Off 145

Be Where You Say You're Going to Be 151

Get Down on Their Level 157

Hear What They Are Saying 161

Quality Over Quantity 171

Let Them Lead 177

Roughhousing 183

Feel the Parenting Burn 191

Conclusion 199

INTRODUCTION

Didn't your mother ever tell you not to judge a book by its cover?

And yet, I bet you judged this book by its cover.

So let me tell you how it got its name.

It all started in my previous life as a college professor in a course I routinely taught, Applied Sport Psychology.

It was 9:30am on a Thursday in January in Northwest Ohio—think cold, gray, and windy—and once again 33 college students crammed into a room meant for 32. "Coach," my co-instructor, a commanding presence mostly due to his 6'5" stature and broad swimmer's shoulders, sat in the front of the room, refusing to stand because he didn't want to "tower" over me and intimidate the students more than he already did.

He didn't mean to intimidate them, but nonetheless, he did.

I claimed center stage and started the class in my regular way:

"Good morning! How is everyone doing today?"

I gauged the sleepiness level of the 33 college students—one level above comatose—so I mentally adjusted my energy level and began lecturing.

"Sport Psychology is the subdiscipline of Psychology that not only focuses on sports, but performance. It's all about developing the mental skills to perform at the highest level that you possibly can. Can anyone tell me the importance of practicing mental skills when it comes to performance?"

The 33 students all did what college students do: darted their eyes from the professor to their desks ...because, if you didn't already know this, the empty desk totally has the answers they're looking for! I knew the majority of them were thinking, "Don't make eye contact! Don't make eye contact! Pretend you're writing or pondering."

Coach threw his arms in the air, leaned back in his seat, and sighed exasperatedly,

"*Did you all read?*"

And, again, the students' eyes shot back to their desks because they were being called out on not completing a course expectation—to read the assigned reading PRIOR to coming to class.

I knew the answer to Coach's question, "*NOPE!*"

Why did I know this?

Well, because college students don't read textbooks! Textbooks are long, dry, and boring. And reading for class can't compete with Netflix, scrolling through TikTok, or ordering Chipotle from Uber Eats. There's no competition...reading a textbook loses every time!

Fast forward two years, to a slightly bigger room, and it was syllabus day*. Coach sat in his chair in the front of the room as I covered some basics of the course. We reached the required text section of the syllabus, and immediately Coach shot out of his chair.

He claimed center stage with what, compared to his large

---

*Syllabus Day—the first day of a college course. I honored syllabus day and all of its glory—meaning, I covered what was on the syllabus, did a brief relationship building activity, and then sent the students on their merry ways! They loved me for it! Whereas, my editor, an English professor, silently judged me for it.

physical stature, appeared to be a mini book (no more textbooks for us, we learned our lesson) and held it out in front of him. He paused until all eyes were on him.

Coach belted out from his diaphragm in a firm authoritative coach's voice,

> "And there are ABSOLUTELY no excuses for not reading this book before you come to class! It's such a quick read that you could read it in the time it takes you to poop."

And who says you don't learn anything in college?

This book will not be your typical parenting book. There will not be long chapters talking all about developmental theory or citing all the research. Again, these things, unless you're a scientist, a nerd or both (like me), are long, dry, and BORING.

Ain't nobody got time for long explanations.

It will literally* be something that you can read while you poop. Because, let's be real, the amount of time that it takes you to poop is about the amount of free time you have to become an intentional parent.

The teachings of this book will be real life stories told in a humorous and relatable way (think "parenting fails") with strategies that you can read, understand, and apply in the time that it takes you to poop. And maybe wait until after you wash your hands before putting them into practice. Just saying!

And if you're regular, and poop once a day, well, then you'll have learned 29 new parenting skills in the next month. And if

---

*Whenever I use this word, please, please, please, use Rob Lowe's voice from Parks and Rec.

you're a typical dad who takes 45 minutes to poop, you might be able to learn all 29 in 5 days.

The 29 practical tips are categorized into three sections: the fundamentals, high expectations, and the warm and fuzzies because the foundational principle guiding this book is something I learned from my parents and is well supported by scientific research:

Children thrive when their parents raise them with high expectations within the context of the warm and fuzzies.

This book is for you, if you simply want:

 To learn how to be an intentional parent

 To know if you are doing too much, or maybe not enough

 To have your child listen to you

 To have a more peaceful home—with you or your child screaming less

 Damn it, if you just want to be left alone so that you CAN poop in peace...

Believe me, I get it!

Mom of twin seven-year-olds and a five-year-old here. Anyone with at least one child under 12 years of age, desires these things. I know, I do.

So, find your porcelain throne and get on your way to becoming a more intentional parent, one poop at a time.

THE FUNDAMENTALS

ALL IS NOT LOST

A text conversation with my dear friend, Harriette:

> H: "I had dinner last night with my parents and we processed more of this stuff with Eddie [10-year-old, boy]. That's what's really been weighing on my heart. It's hard not to look at where he is now and feel like it's always going to be this way with him."

I hopped on YouTube, found Darius Rucker's "It Won't Be Like This for Long*" video, and sent it to her.

> H: "This song always makes me cry!!! I guess I'm just so scared he's going to be like his dad [Carl]. Carl's a narcissist, and so is his dad. And Eddie's with both of them right now."
>
> A: "Break down 'narcissist' into behaviors. Then we can work on reinforcing Eddie's good behaviors and punishing Eddie's bad behaviors."
>
> H: "That's so good—I think I get fatalistic because I look at it as a mindset and not as behaviors. I have so much trouble dealing with the lying because I end up praising him for something that I find out later wasn't true."
>
> A: "Let's focus on modifying behavior. You have plenty of time before his personality is set, which happens around 25 years of age."
>
> H: "You have no idea how much that just boosted me! Wow, I needed to hear that. All I keep hearing is how critical the first 7 years are, and I'm sitting over here feeling like I blew it!

---

*"And when he drops her off at preschool…She's clinging to his leg …
The teacher peels her off of him … He says what can I do …
She says now don't you worry … This will only last a week or two …
It wont be like this for long"

That definitely helps me stay focused."

A: *"I'm glad. You didn't blow it. You have plenty of time."*

H: *"Thanks so much for talking me down.
I feel like I can do this again. You're amazing!"*

One of the perks of being my family member or friend is you get immediate help with all family matters. Harriette experienced something that most, if not all, parents experience—wondering whether what they're doing is going to cause permanent damage to their child. I get it. But rest assured, the chances are if you're taking the time and reading a parenting book (I assume you didn't mistakenly think this was a book on how to poop better), then you're not causing permanent damage. Children can be resilient if we let them be. And given this book is written for parents who have children between the ages of 3-12, you, like Harriette, have plenty of time to turn it around.

And if you have teenagers, Godspeed and keep tequila handy!

Humans sometimes get caught up in labeling. This is what Harriette was doing when she labeled Carl a narcissist. But when parenting, labeling does us no good. It can serve as a self-fulfilling prophecy for our children, and we don't want that. Whether or not you believe people can change, please know children CAN change with modifications to their environment—aka how they're parented.

I want you to remember something that my husband's Aunt Alice told me when she was teaching me to water ski: "Never let go of the rope—you can always recover!" It was something the person who taught her how to water ski said to her.

Now, it isn't really true when it comes to water skiing, because sometimes you should let go of the rope— a dislocated shoulder is no bueno— and start fresh on the next run.

But in parenting, it's sound advice: "Never let go, you can always recover."

It doesn't matter what you did last year, last month, or even within the last five minutes.

You can always recover as a parent.

So, let's pretend we're friends. And now you have access to your own clinical child psychologist who has no other desire than to see more intentional parents who raise well-adjusted adults who can form strong attachments and strong marriages who then become more intentional parents and raise the next generation of well-adjusted adults.

Ooh! I love me some exponential benefits!

My dear friend, take my hand...

And continually repeat:

 All is not lost.

 Be kind.

 Breathe.

 Make the next parenting moment better than the last.

 I can always recover.

Now, from here on out, let's focus on modifying your child's behaviors to make life for everyone much more enjoyable.

And that's exactly what happened with Harriette and Eddie.

Harriette and I did a zoom call a few months after our text message exchange. She told me how Eddie had turned his behaviors around, wasn't lying (at least not to her knowledge) anymore, and that their relationship was stronger than it ever had been.

Harriette recovered and you can too, let me teach you how.

YOU CAN'T PARENT FROM THE COUCH

A mother, Christy, and her five-year-old adorable little girl, Josie, walked into my office for their initial session. Seventy-five minutes later, Christy and I had this conversation.

> *"Okay, Christy, based on what you're telling me, it seems like Josie meets criteria for Oppositional Defiant Disorder, or ODD.*
>
> *"The big clue for ODD is that, at least according to Mrs. Flowers, Josie is a well-behaved student in the kindergarten classroom. She is not seeing any of the problem behaviors you've described in the classroom. The great thing is that ODD is treatable with parent training and most of my clients see a significant reduction of symptoms in about eight sessions. What questions do you have?"*
>
> *"Oppositional Defiant Disorder?"*
>
> *"Yes, but in about two months, with you learning effective parenting practices, we can have her no longer meeting criteria. How does that sound?"*
>
> *"That sounds good to me. Thank you."*

Fast forward two weeks.

> *"Andrea, I did exactly what you told me to do, but it didn't work. I praised her A LOT, but she still didn't do what I told her to do."*
>
> *"Hmm. I bet that's very frustrating. Okay, let's see if we can figure out what's going on. So, whenever Josie did something*

you wanted her to do more of, you praised her using specific and concrete statements?*"

"Yeah."

"And when she did something you didn't want her to do, you didn't pay her any attention*, but then praised her the second she started doing the behavior you wanted her to do?"

"Yeah."

"Hmm...that's strange. Please tell me about two specific times, one when you praised her and one when you ignored her."

"Really?! What's that gonna do?"

"It's going to give me some insight on what adjustments we need to make."

"Argh! Fine! Okay, one time she was coloring, and I told her, 'Good job.' Another time she was running in the house, which I HATE because it vibrates the floor and it's so loud, so I reminded her to walk."

I think to myself: That's not exactly what I said, but this is only her second session. I'm not going to push too much, yet.

Instead, I advised, "Christy, it seems like you're really trying to make positive changes. For this next week, let's continue to catch her being good and ignore all behaviors we don't want her to do. So, a small tweak to the example you gave would be to praise her when she is coloring by herself in the house and ignore when she is running. Can you try that this week?"

"Yeah."

---

*Stay tuned! Catch and Ignore talks about these.

Another session passed in a similar way—Christy telling me the effective parenting techniques are not effective, and me wondering what I was doing wrong.

At this point, I had NEVER experienced a client with such terrible results. I talked with my supervisor at the time about it, and she suggested we ask a case manager to help.

A case manager is any employee within the agency who collaborates with therapists, ensuring what we're suggesting in session is being executed in the home.

Two weeks later, I met with Tanesha, Christy's case manager.

"Hey Tanesha! Thank you so much for helping with Christy and Josie. I'm anxious to hear what you discovered."

"Well... Christy is doing what you've told her to do...just from the couch."

Tanesha delivered the revelation with a sassy face.

My head falls backwards in exasperation.

"What?!"

"YEP! Christy lays on the couch, watches TV, and regardless of where Josie is, yells at her to do things. All from the couch.

"Christy praises Josie as long as Josie is in the living room, which is rare, AND it's during a commercial break (remember, this story took place when I was in grad school, Netflix was the only streaming service available, and this family was living in poverty, so didn't have Netflix). *The praise looks something like, 'Good girl.'"*

"How does Josie respond?"

"Josie stops what she is doing in a bedroom and walks to the doorway of the living room and asks her mom, 'What?' Christy shoos her away because she's watching General Hospital and can't miss a single line."

"Okay...that's not what I had in mind when I instructed her to praise Josie's desirable behavior. And what about ignoring Josie's undesirable behavior?"

"Oh, she ignores Josie, but that's Christy's default. Not because she's ignoring the behavior she doesn't want Josie to do."

"Aggg! Maybe that's my fault!? I didn't think I needed to tell Christy that she actually needed to be in the same room, engage, AND interact with Josie for these parenting practices to work. Who woulda thought? That's my bad. Silly me."

As I face palmed.

The tips in this book work.

But here is the key: you must use them and be engaged with your child. Parenting is not easy at first. It's what I call a front-loaded activity, not a passive one. You must exert a lot of effort and energy at the beginning, but then later you expend less energy and time, AND see results.

Think of it like cruise control. First, your car revs high and uses a lot of gas to get you to the speed you want to be at. And when you push the set button, what happens? You cruise[*]!

What causes you to cruise?

---

[*]Do you hear it? Florida Georgia Line and Nelly's song, *Cruise*! By following the parenting pointers in this book, my goal is that you and your child have a better fate than FGL's...

The car is now going at a consistent speed.

What causes you to cruise when parenting? Parenting becomes second nature. It'll get easier the more you follow the parenting tips in this book, the more you're consistent.

It's just like riding a bike. At first you have no idea what you're doing, but then once you get the hang of it, you can do other things. But at first it requires a lot, if not ALL of your attention. I promise it will not always be like this. You will have days where you're second guessing yourself, but using these tips are so worth it.

Trust me.

If, after reading the last few paragraphs, you're thinking, "Nah! Hard pass! That's too much work for me. I'm a Christy!" that's okay—do you, Boo! But then maybe you should stop reading this book and go search for this one I once saw in Target titled, "Horizontal Parenting: How to Entertain Your Kid Lying Down." I immediately cringed and died a little inside.

Please know, there'll be times when you're oh so very tempted to parent from the couch. And don't get me wrong, there'll be days when you have to (i.e., you're sick, pregnant, just birthed a human, injured, or damn it, you just need a 15-minute break, etc).

But, if after reading about how parenting is a front-loaded activity, you're like, "Give it to me! I want all of it! I'm all in!" then...

I want you to try this:

 Remind yourself that parenting is a front-loaded activity.

Say, "I'm choosing my hard now instead of later." This is what's called a coping thought. I encourage them all the time.

 Continue reading and putting the parenting tips into practice.

And hopefully you and your child will have a better fate than Christy and Josie–which I don't know what happened to them, because they quit coming to therapy.

I can only hope that Christy realized I wasn't the best fit for her (as a tank top I own says, "I'm not for everyone"), chose to go to a different therapist (doubtful, but a woman can dream), got up off the couch, and parented Josie with high expectations within the context of warm and fuzzies.

CONSISTENCY, CONSISTENCY, CONSISTENCY

Liam, a ten-year-old boy, and his parents, Mitch and Cameron sat down – Cameron between her son and husband.

I immediately picked up on some tension. I wrongly assumed the tension was due to last week's session where Liam's word choice and body language made Mitch and me concerned that Liam had been abused at a summer camp.

Let me pause here, and say that thankfully Liam wasn't, but we didn't learn that until later.

> "Liam, last week was intense, and I'm not entirely sure we ever figured out what you were trying to tell dad and me, but what would you like to focus on this week?"

He hesitated and looked at Cameron.

Cameron looked back and said,

> "I think I know what you want to talk about, but I'm not going to say it. You have to."

Liam pulled his oversized stocking cap down over his eyes. He removed it from his moistened eyes. He paused.

Not being able to stand the uncomfortableness her son felt, Cameron jumped in and said,

> "Didn't you want to talk about trust and your dad?"

Liam shot Cameron the death stare and, then again, pulled his stocking cap down over his eyes.

This time, when he removed his hat from his eyes, his eyes were closed and he lamented, while looking at Mitch,

"*I don't trust you.*"

All the air in the room vanished. This was definitely not what I was expecting, and I know for damn sure Mitch, this loving and engaged yet military discipline father, wasn't either. If I could read minds*, Mitch would most likely have been thinking, "He doesn't trust me? The US military trusts me, but my son doesn't? How could that even be a thing?"

I paused momentarily, gave Liam a little bit of time to gather his thoughts and elaborate on what he meant by "I don't trust you," and in that pause the tension in the room thickened.

Cameron and I realized Liam wasn't expanding on the bomb he just dropped. Cameron shot me a look and I asked Liam,

"*What makes you say that you can't trust your dad?*"

"*I never know how he's going to react when he comes home after being gone for 8 weeks. Sometimes he flies off the handle when I talk back. But other times he's cool, calm, and collected. I freeze.*"

Mitch, utterly confused by his son's perception of him, replied with,

"*I don't agree. Disrespecting me is never acceptable. And I'm sure I consistently let you know that.*"

Mitch was about to continue his closing argument, but Cameron interrupted.

---

*Which some people think I can, but here's my secret, and what I can actually do, I'm extremely observant, perceptive, and I read body language REALLY well! My editor says I'm spooky this way.

"You're inconsistent. There are times that I don't know why you're reacting the way you're reacting, but if you do it to me, I look at you and call you out on your bullshit. He's your son. He can't. He doesn't have the power. You're my equal, I can call you out, he's powerless in your and his relationship."

We humans love us some consistency! So, let me put this in a language you parents, aka "adults," can understand. Many of us have bosses. And our bosses are humans. Therefore, they all fall on a continuum of how consistent they are. When our bosses are consistent, we are mentally and emotionally good. We know exactly what they expect from us.

But now, think of a time when a boss or someone who had power over you, was inconsistent. They told you one thing and then completely flipped and expected the complete opposite. I'm sure no one reading this book has EVER experienced that. BAA HAA HA! As Cher from the wonderful 90's movie, *Clueless*, would say, "As if!"

We've all experienced this and, chances are, you didn't handle it well mentally and emotionally. You most likely became frustrated, angry, or irate.

Why?

Because humans don't do well with inconsistency. We thrive on consistency. We like routines, and if you're one of those people who laments that you don't do routines, Malarkey! I would question whether you're thriving as well as you could if you simply gave into the "man" and developed a consistent routine.

Children are no different. They, too, thrive on consistency.

And I truly believe consistency is the cornerstone of all parenting. If you take nothing else away from this book, or if you don't finish it, please remember this, consistency is the cornerstone of all parenting.

If you want to work on one thing and only one thing as a parent—shit, as a human—become more consistent. In the grand scheme of parenting, I would rather have a neglectful parent—a parent who does not give a damn about their child, but is consistently neglectful—than a parent who is inconsistently loving and warm. There is a lot of attachment theory and developmental psychology knowledge to back this up, but again, I promised I wouldn't bore you with that.

Think of the other 28 practical tips in this book as building blocks. Each one will help construct the parenting wall of your fortress*. Before you can lay that particular building block down, you must consistently execute that parenting tip. It has to become second nature.

Steps to becoming more consistent in parenting:

 Read through this book

 Every night, spend 5 minutes reflecting on your parenting by writing answers to these three prompts:
1. What did I do well today?
2. What could I have improved on today?
3. What joy did I receive today from my child?

 Once you've read the book, look at your improvement areas (question 2), and create a list of areas you could improve your parenting

---

*See my TEDx talk, "From Murder to Mission: How I Found My Life's Calling." Available on YouTube.

Choose one area, find the practical tip that is most likely to help, and reread that parenting tip

 Implement that parenting tip every day for 10 days or until it becomes second nature. Then . . .

 Build: choose the next area, and repeat the two previous steps

---

Liam, Mitch, and Cameron are one of my therapy success stories. Liam put in the work and completed therapy. Mitch continues to work on becoming more consistent as a parent, because when it comes to consistency, just like with parenting, it's never ending. You can always add another building block to the parenting wall of your fortress.

ADAPT!

Jim, my husband, contemplated being a stay-at-home dad.

Until…we had twins and he got stir crazy after 1.5 weeks of paternity leave.

But in 2021, he resigned from one job and had two weeks before his new job started, so he gave being a stay-at-home dad another chance.

Learning from his paternity leave, he predicted he would go stir crazy if he and the now three kids spent too much time at the house. So, he planned outings for most days. You know, the zoo, hikes, parks, active stuff!

One morning, after they hiked, he decided to take the two 4-year-olds and 2-year-old to the grocery store.

He thought, "How hard can it be? Andrea does it all the time."

Poor guy.

Upon arrival, Jim and the kids realized the store didn't have any family carts—you know, the real nice ones, where there's a bench where the twins sit and the regular seat for the youngest. So, he grabbed a regular cart and went about the shopping trip.

The trip turned south real quick.

None of the kids wanted to sit in the cart, so he let them roam, and roaming turned into all out chaos! The three children ran up and down all the aisles. Laughing! Hoopin' and hollerin'! Having the grandest time! Living their best little hellion lives!

People inundated Jim with looks of sympathy, made my favorite comment of all time, "Wow! You have your hands full," and reassured him that it would get easier.

Later that night, Jim recounted the story to me. "I was one of 'those people*,' Andrea. I felt defeated. I even tried to redirect them by buying them popcorn chicken. But nothing worked. I simply tried to get out of the store as fast as humanly possible... ."

I'm sure no one reading this book is thinking "Been there, done that, got the t-shirt!"

When I heard this, I glared at our kids and asked them with a hand on my hip,

"Did you behave like this?"

All three of them looked at me and slowly nodded their heads — acknowledging they did.

"Is this how you're expected to behave in the grocery store?"

And each of them smiled slyly and said, *"Noooo."*

Our children are not saints. There's a reason Jim and I have

*You know the people we are talking about—the people who allow their children to run chaotically around stores without any discipline.

labeled them a Sassafras, a Rascal, and a Troublemaker. These labels identify prominent aspects of their personalities.

They knew they weren't supposed to act like that, but they chose to act that way because their father allowed them to act like that.

Here's a fact about children: when given the opportunity, they'll act like savages—*Lord of the Flies* style! It's our responsibility as parents to direct them. So let's help prevent you from earning a second, third, fourth, or whatever number t-shirt.

When the typical conditions where your children behave like angels changes aka no amazingly-awesome-can't-shop-without-if-you-have-three-young-children-cart, then adapt.

Adaptability!

Jean Piaget, a big name in Developmental Psychology, defined intelligence as your ability to adapt.

I want you to become a parent who adapts no matter the conditions. My husband did not have the cart. So, if he wanted our typically well-behaved children to go grocery shopping with him, then he needed to lay out new expectations for the children.

That looks like this:

Go off to the side and pull the children into a huddle, bend down so that you're at their level, and say, "Alright. The cart we typically use is not available. And that sucks, but here's what we're going to do. Who wants to sit in the high up seat where you can see everything?" If you didn't already know this, a good portion of parenting is selling what you're wanting them to do.

If no one volunteers, then follow up with, "Okay, all three of you are expected to walk with a hand on the cart (demonstrate it). We're going to use our inside voices. We're going to get what we came to get." Give each child an item that they must remember throughout the store—it gives them something productive to focus on.

"And if you three keep one hand on the cart at all times and use inside voices, then each of you will earn a treat!" The treat can be whatever your family rewards (See Positive Reinforcement, Your First Line of Defense) with, ours is typically a doughnut or a ride on Sandy the Horse at Meijer.

How did I come up with this?

Problem solving! I'm convinced that adaptability is 88% (I made this stat up) problem solving. And if adaptability is core to being an intentional parent, well then, we need to improve your problem-solving skills.

I think this is SO important that I've inserted an exercise for you all to complete.

Do the exercise! Don't cheat and flip ahead.

"You'll only be cheating yourself!*"

---

*Oh no! I used one of my father's favorite "dadisms" in my parenting book...

Here are the basic steps:

STEP 1: Identify the problem.

_____

STEP 2: List all solutions without judgment. This is the most challenging step for most people. I want you to get creative and think outside the box.

_____
_____
_____
_____
_____
_____
_____
_____

Step 3: Evaluate each solution on a 1-10 scale. 1-being it wouldn't solve the problem and it may cause more headache. 10-being it's 95% (another made up stat) sure to solve the problem and would cause little to no additional headache.

STEP 4: Try out the highest ranked solution. If it doesn't work, then work your way down the list until you've solved the damn problem, or it resolved itself.

"Answers"

Answers are in quotations because there's an infinite number of ways to solve any problem. There's not one right answer, just like there is not just one right way to parent. I preach my techniques because they have worked for myself and hundreds of clients.

 Identify the problem:

No carts, the kids are tired and hungry, and I want to go grocery shopping.

 List all solutions without judgment:

- Throw two kids over your shoulders, the other under your arm pit, and leave.
- Forget a cart. Give each kid a basket.
- Put two kids in the main compartment of the cart and the third up top.
- Allow the children to run around like little hellions and shoulder shrug.
- Yank their arms and yell non-stop at them.
- Pretend you don't know whose kids these are and shop by yourself.

- Huddle the children and set a new game plan.
- Walk out, leaving the children behind. They're Meijer's problem now.
- Grab a basket and create a human line by holding their hands.
- Initiate a game like follow the leader.

 Evaluate each solution on a 1-10 scale:

4/10   Throw two kids over your shoulders, the other under your arm pit, and leave. (You escaped the embarrassment, but you don't get any groceries.)

6/10   Forget a cart. Give each kid a basket. (Each child has something to occupy their focus. They feel like they are being included. But they're still walking by themselves and now you have given them props to hit each other and others with, "accidentally," of course!)

9/10   Put two kids in the main compartment of the cart and the third up top. (The children are contained. You can shop. They get to ride because remember they're tired and hungry. But they may complain about the comfort level in the main compartment of the cart.)

5/10   Allow the children to run around like little hellions and shoulder shrug. (This worked okay for Jim. No one got hurt—other than Jim's ego and feelings. He got to shop.)

2/10   Yank their arms and yell non-stop at them. (Yanking their arms? Borderline physical abuse... and I never advocate for yelling at your children non-stop.)

3/10   Pretend you don't know whose kids these are and shop by yourself. (I mean you do get your shopping done, but pretending your children aren't yours is really bad for their attachment to you!)

10/10 Huddle the children and set a new game plan. (This is obviously the best option because it is what I suggested earlier! DUH!)

1/10   Walk out, leaving the children behind. They're Meijer's problem now. (Um...child abandonment...need I say more????)

8/10   Grab a basket and create a human line by holding their hands. (One basket to manage. Get to shop. And holding their hands is a great way to connect and contain them.)

7/10   Initiate a game like follow the leader. (Focuses the children's attention. It's fun. May wear off quickly.)

 Try out the highest ranked solution:

Huddle the children and set a new game plan.

Once you get real good at this parenting skill, you've upped your parenting IQ, and it's a game changer, not only in parenting, but in all aspects of life.

Jim has learned from his grocery shopping mistake, some may say he was "traumatized" by this experience.

Therefore, he now goes grocery shopping by himself on Sundays and I play with the kids at home.

ONE SIZE DOESN'T FIT ALL

"What do you mean I can't parent all my children the same?" a deflated dad of three skeptically asked me.

"You and Bethany have Tyson [9-year-old], who has been diagnosed with a sensory processing disorder which requires physical, occupational, and speech therapy, and who is also highly perfectionistic. Then y'all have Natalia [7-year-old] who is easy, agreeable, quiet, and wicked smart. And to round it out, there's Taylor [5-year-old] who is a feisty firecracker with a personality to match. Three very different personalities."

"You're tellin' me! And so, you're saying Bethany and me, but mostly me, must learn three different parenting styles?!"

"Not three different styles, per say. You only need one style, but how you execute the style changes depending on which child you're parenting."

"ANDREA! I'm exhausted just thinking about it."

"I know it seems like that, but once you and Bethany get the parenting fundamentals down, tweaking the execution is a hell of a lot easier! Scout's honor."

I awkwardly made a three-finger gesture, uncertain whether I did it correctly.

Greg laughed.

"You got it right, but I don't know if I believe you... I'm pretty sure writing and defending my master's thesis was easier than parenting these three, um...maniacs! Remind me again, why I chose to be a stay-at-home dad?"

Greg raises his hands, palms facing up, indicating that he doesn't know.

I giggled.

"Um, Greg, wasn't your thesis on some super complicated aspect of human genetics?"

Greg chuckled.

"Yeah..."

"And correct me if I'm wrong, you and Bethany decided on you being a stay-at-home dad because her schedule was going to get crazy hectic when she was named the Athletic Director, after Natalia was born, and the number of Tyson's doctors' appointments grew exponentially. And then y'all were 'blessed' with Taylor..."

"Yeah, Taylor is what you get when you mix DayQuil and a bottle of Jose Cuervo[*]."

We laughed because we both know what it's like to be blessed with a third child who you didn't plan on having but adds so much to your family. For the record, my husband and I didn't get blessed with our third by mixing DayQuil and tequila.

"Let's focus! Okay, I mean, you're kinda smart, Greg. At some level you must have known, given their three very different personalities, they can't all be parented the same. I mean c'mon. You and Bethany named your three children, Tyson, Natalia, and Taylor—TNT! BOOM!"

---

[*]And for all my non-Mexican readers, this is a terrible tequila choice, as is Patrón.

"You right." Greg admitted.

"Of course I am! Now, how about we get you thriving as a stay-at-home dad?!"

"Thriving sounds a heck of a lot better than what we're doing—surviving...barely."

There's no one size fits all solution—unfortunately! It's true--there's no such thing as a parenting manual; if there was, unfortunately for me, you would've bought that one over this parenting book. But if you can identify which of these three children your child most resembles, then, maybe, just maybe, you can create your own parenting manual.

A huge concept in the world of parenting is "goodness of fit." What that means is that the execution of the parenting style needs to match the child's personality. You may be thinking, "Why the hell, then, are you writing a parenting book, if not all kids are the same?"

The parenting tips are the same, but the execution needs to be tweaked.

This concept is super challenging because we learn a lot on the job as a parent and with the first child. You figure it out and then BAM! Your next child requires you to tweak the execution of the same parenting practices. The rules change. We're like rats who've learned that if we press this lever, we get food. But then one day, the food doesn't come. We're left there yelling, "WTF!" and breaking the lever out of frustration.

So, now you know that you need to adjust, I'm sure you're asking "what does that look like?" Well, you're in luck because

I have a handy-dandy tool on the next page to help.

Here's what you do:

 Look at the diagram

 Choose whether your child is most like Tyson, Natalia or Taylor

 Follow the guidelines in the bottom box for that particular child

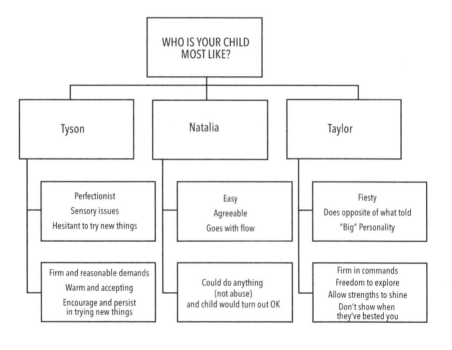

Therapy Success Story!

Greg and Bethany learned how to adapt the execution of the parenting tips to their three very different children and now they're thriving as a family, and not simply surviving.

GIVE THEM JUST ENOUGH

"MAMA!"

Jim walked into the bathroom to see what any of our three children needed, given they're shouting for me.

He got their typical reaction, *"NO! MAMA!"*

Jim walked from the bathroom, a sly smile, looked at me and said, "Mama!" He shrugged his shoulders and continued doing whatever it was he was doing before one of our stubborn children shouted for me. This was definitely one of the times when I'm envious of my husband's less-connected relationship with our children. Now, don't get it twisted—he is an engaged father —but if you asked each of them who they loved more, they would tell you, "Mama."

I begrudgingly stopped whatever I was doing and walked to the bathroom.

"Yes, sweetie? What do you need?"

"I pooped!"

"That's great! Do you need me to wipe your butt?"

"Yes, please."

I stroll over, grab a wipe, have the child lean forward, and wipe the small amount of poop from their butt, all while thinking, "He/she could have done this all by themselves. I didn't need to stop doing what I was doing to wipe their ass."

I gave myself a second and thought about how to verbalize this thought in a way that was child-friendly and wouldn't ding the relationship.

"Honey, there wasn't a lot of poop. You can wipe your own butt. Please try to wipe your own butt before you call me to help next time, okay?"

"Okay, mama."

Let's pause here and do the dissolve sound from *Wayne's World* and explore how this very scene would have played out differently had I not been home and it solely would have been Jim alone with the three kids.

"Daddy!"

Jim walked into the bathroom to see what the child wanted.

"Yes, what is it?"

"I pooped!"

"That's great! Wipe your butt and wash your hands."

"But, Daddy. I need help wiping my butt."

"No, you don't. I've seen you wipe your own butt before. You can do it again."

"Daddy! ARGH!"

"I'm not doing something for you that you can do all by yourself. If you want, I will check after you wipe to make sure you got all the poop."

"Hurumph! Fine!"

The child grabbed toilet paper from the roll, waded it up, and wiped their own butt.

Jim checks the child's butt.

"All clean. Great job. See. You can do it all by yourself."

In under 30 seconds, Jim returned to what he was doing prior to being called to the porcelain panic room. Our child, feeling accomplished, shoulders high, chest out, washed their hands and then went back to playing.

There's one and only one parenting skill that my husband, Jim, is far superior at than me—scaffolding. Scaffolding is providing your child with just enough assistance so that they can successfully complete the task all by themselves. Jim scaffolded when he said he would check their butt after they wiped.

Not allowing your children to do things makes you a slave to their "needs." I don't know about you, but I don't want to be a slave to my child's "needs." Don't get me wrong, I want to meet their needs—you did just finish a whole chapter on adapting to the kids—but I'm purposefully putting "needs" in quotations.

Be mindful of your own language: differentiate a need from a want.

A need is something you need to survive and/or thrive. A want is a nice-to-have-but-you're-not-going-to-die-if-you-don't-get-it.

Your child will not die if you encourage them to practice trial and error, making mistakes, failing, and embracing the suck and struggle. They will actually become the opposite of dead—resilient. You will build agency in them: the belief that they can do things themselves.

Success is a terrible teacher. So is doing everything for your child. That's called being a snowplow parent. Think of the last time you succeeded. What did you learn?

Nothing. Now, think of the last time you failed? What did you learn? Everything.

You may be thinking, "But Dr. Dre. I don't have time to scaffold! We need to get out the door right now!" and you may say, "Oh, just let me do it!"

I get all this. I tell myself the same things. I say the same things.

But slow the hell down. Again, I'm telling myself this as much as I am telling you all. In the moment, ask yourself "Is it more important to be early or on time to everything OR for your child to develop independence?"

Yes, sometimes the answer to this question will be the former, but it shouldn't always be. If it is, then you may be a… (looks both ways, makes sure no one is around, and then whispers) helicopter parent.

If you find yourself behaving like a snowplow, helicopter, or bulldozer parent, well then, practicing scaffolding is the best way to stop that behavior.

How to practice scaffolding:

 When you want to bust in and do it for your child, Stop!

 Use a coping thought, such as, "If I want my child to be independent, I must let them learn to do things for themselves."

Evaluate the skill the child is working on.

 Encourage (you know, force) them to do it themselves.

 Provide help when and where they need it. But be sure to let them struggle. Struggling is good for kids in so many ways.

 Help them cope with the struggle: Breaths. Slowing down. Thinking about what the next step is.

 Remember to treat your child's behavior like Play-Doh*—shape it!

 Once they accomplish it, praise the hell out of 'em.

Jim continues to be stronger at making our children do things for themselves. Scaffolding is a parenting skill I will continue and probably always struggle with. It's something I have to catch myself, pause, take a breath, encourage them to do the behavior themselves, and grin and bear the extremely long time it takes them to complete a task I could have done in half the time.

*You'll learn this later in the book.

SENTENCING YOUR CHILD TO A LIFE IN YOUR BASEMENT

I flopped down on a chair in Beth's office. The whole exasperated shebang: my arms hung on either side, my head felt too heavy to hold up, and my legs appeared to be noodles.

Beth stopped what she was doing and assumed her clinical psychologist pose.

"What's going on, Andrea?"

"It's this mom, Beth. I just can't."

"Draco's mom?"

Not having the energy to say anything or nod my head, I simply closed my eyes—communicating that Beth guessed the mom who exhausted me.

"OK. Bring me up to date on...what was her name again?"

"Narcissa." Eye roll and all.

Beth nodded and I began recapping my journey with Draco, Narcissa, and Lucius, Draco's father.

> *"Draco, a nine-year old male, was referred for a learning disability assessment due to his parents' concerns of him struggling in school. Draco has an older sister. Narcissa is a stay-at-home mom. And Lucius is a businessman who earns a whopping $250,000 a year.*
>
> *"The combination of the results did not suggest a learning disability—therefore, we started exploring alternative explanations.*

"Narcissa voiced concerns that Draco was being bullied. I went and observed Draco at school and met with his teachers. And..."

PLOT TWIST! Draco wasn't being bullied—he was the bully.

"When I conveyed this information to Narcissa and Lucius, they were in disbelief that their son would be so terrible, but willing to have Draco try therapy.

We created a beautiful treatment plan. Draco and I got only one session under our belts before the incessant phone calls from Narcissa started.

She calls and emails me EVERY single day—questioning whether this is the best treatment option for her dear Draco. I try to reassure her and provide her with resources and evidence, but it's a lot, Beth. It's like she is trying to control me and EVERYTHING that I do in my sessions. It's suffocating."

"Suffocating you say?"

"Yes, like I can't breathe."

"Hence, your current state?!"

"Haha! Yeah..."

"Okay, tell me about how Narcissa is with Draco and his sister at home."

"Oh my goodness, Beth. She plans every minute of their day. She is like a lurking drill sergeant. She wakes Draco and his sister up, feeds them breakfast, picks out their clothes for school, for all I know she might actually put the clothes on them, BAA HAA HA! She drives them to and from school. She then picks them up. Once they get home, Draco and his sister get 5 minutes and 32 seconds to unwind with pre-approved activities."

Beth laughed at my exaggeration.

I continued detailing Narcissa's insane overparenting:

> "Draco and his sister complete their homework, clean up for dinner, eat dinner as a family, and then engage in nighttime activities where Narcissa supervises everything Draco does, and then it's off to bed. I think I got everything."
>
> "And does Narcissa allow any flexibility?"
>
> "Haha! You're funny, Beth. No. No flexibility whatsoever."
>
> "So, what I hear you saying is that every single minute of Draco's day is planned, controlled, and supervised by Narcissa?"
>
> "Yes."
>
> "Now, put yourself in Draco's shoes. What would you feel if every second of your life was planned, controlled, and supervised by your mother?"

The light bulb went off.

> "Suffocated."
>
> "The same thing you're feeling because of Narcissa right now, correct?"
>
> "Probably."
>
> "What you're currently feeling is what Draco experiences day in and day out. And Andrea, you have just learned an important lesson as a clinical psychologist, countertransference* is your friend. Pay attention to it; it gives great insight into what people in your client's life experience when they interact with this client."

---

*Countertransference is the feelings that clinical psychologists and other mental health providers may experience in response to how their clients behave.

And then two words I thought I'd never utter came out of my mouth,

"*Poor Draco.*"

Do you engage in any of the following behaviors:

- ☐ Supervise or monitor your child's independent play
- ☐ Pick out your child's clothing
- ☐ Check all your child's homework
- ☐ Supervise or monitor all play dates*
- ☐ Plan all activities
- ☐ Cut up all your child's food into bite size pieces (when no longer age appropriate)
- ☐ Try to solve their problems for them
- ☐ Step in at the first sign of peer conflict
- ☐ Prevent or minimize any obstacles
- ☐ Try to put your child in a better emotional state whenever they're down.

If you endorsed numerous behaviors, chances are you may be... wait for it...a helicopter parent. OR a bulldozer parent. OR a snowplow parent. Choose your favorite term.

Dun Dun Dun!

You might be defending yourself, saying something along the lines of, "I just want what's best for my child. Is that a crime?!"

---

*If I'm honest with myself, I "struggle" with this one. I like my kids. And I like to play. I'm the fun parent. And truthfully, I'd rather play with the kids than talk with the other parents....maybe that's why I don't have very many mom friends.

No, it most certainly is not a crime, but you're preventing your child from developing both independence and autonomy. These characteristics are important to develop, especially in the United States given that our 'Murica! culture is all about people doing things by themselves. We aren't very forgiving or understanding of those that rely on others.

Culture aside, do you want your child living in your basement when they're 40 years old? If so, then skip the rest of this parenting tip and continue overparenting. But you're making your life as a parent so much more challenging.

For instance, what could you get off your to do list if you weren't overparenting?

How many times have you heard yourself or a loved one say, "I just can't get anything done around the house when the kids are home."

Why?

Because whoever said that is, overparenting.

You're doing too much.

STOP IT!

 Review the overparenting behaviors you marked.

 Look below for quick tweaks on how not to do those behaviors:

Supervise or monitor your child's independent play:
- ☐ Go get tasks on your to do list accomplished. Periodically (every 5 minutes, extend out depending on your child's age) check in on them. Don't have them rely on you for entertainment. Let them be bored.

> Boredom is good. It spawns creativity.

Pick out your child's clothing:

> ☐ Let them choose their own clothing and learn to be okay with how they're dressed. Obviously, there are exceptions to this. Pick out their clothes when they are expected to look nice: weddings, family photos, church, the theatre, etc.

Check all your child's homework:

> ☐ Patience young grasshopper. You'll learn in Tired of Nagging? Use Natural Consequences why this is a bad choice.

Supervise or monitor all play dates:

> ☐ Engage with the other parents. Parents need connection too!

Plan all activities:

> ☐ You'll learn how to address this in the next parenting tip, Stop the Busyness.

Cut up all your child's food into bite size pieces (when no longer age appropriate):

> ☐ Teach them how to cut up their own food once they've shown they can be trusted with a knife.

Try to solve their problems for them:

> ☐ Teach them the problem-solving steps you learned in Adapt! And encourage problem solving by saying, "Hey, let's problem solve this."

Step in at the first sign of peer conflict:

- ☐ Stay out of it unless someone is about to get seriously injured (see caveat in Tired of Nagging? Use Natural Consequences for what your threshold is)

Prevent or minimize any obstacles:

- ☐ Teach them to embrace the suck! Struggling is good for them. It helps them build resiliency. We want our children to be resilient.

Try to put your child in a better emotional state whenever they're down:

- ☐ Lead with empathy. Review "Reflect what your child is saying" from the parenting tip, "Hear What They're Saying"

I'm sad to report that Narcissa stopped bringing Draco to therapy because I didn't allow her to dictate the treatment plan and quite frankly she never accepted the realization that Draco wasn't being bullied and he in fact was the bully.

I take some ownership of this therapy fail because had this case been later in my career, I think I would have done a better job of incorporating and including Narcissa into the treatment planning.

STOP THE BUSYNESS

"Joni, GREAT NEWS!"

Jules, Joni's mom, beamed from ear to ear.

Joni, a nine-year-old, whose two moms brought her in for therapy due to her oppositional and defiant behavior—a child after my own soul—glared at her mom and waited for this supposed great news.

> "I remembered you mentioned tennis. So, guess what! I signed you up for a tennis class!"

Joni's response to her mom's excitement and gesture of love was a seven-year old's equivalent of a side eye. She was none too pleased.

After she stared at her mom for some time, she finally told her in a disdained voice,

> "I'm not doing a tennis class."

With her contempt, Joni shut down the conversation.

As the therapist, I allowed it because in the back of my mind, I was thinking, "Damn it! Don't put her in yet another activity! Let her have some free time."

We revisited the topic the following week.

> "Joni, I think you don't want to do tennis class because it's something new.

Or because you will be in a big group,"

Nic, Joni's mama, suggested.

"NO! I don't want to do tennis class because I DON'T want to do tennis."

Nic came back with,

"Hmm...Joni, well, I think it's one of those reasons. But maybe... it could be because you don't want any more structured activities because those activities eat up some of your free time."

"Some?" Joni retorted.

Joni quickly followed up with,

"When exactly would we fit in yet another class? I already do violin and karate classes.

"And you and mom have all my days scheduled out. I wake up at 6:30am, eat breakfast, practice violin for 30 minutes, practice piano for 30 minutes, 20 minutes of screen time, if I willingly practice violin and piano. Then you ship me off to school for six hours. I come home and then the rest of my evening is filled with more 'productive' pursuits. Latin. Creative writing. And painting. Just to name a few."

"We want what's best for you. Where we grew up, parents scheduled their child's days like this, pushed them, and enrolled them in as many activities as they could in hopes of getting them admitted to a premier preschool—because as you know, it's the way to get into an Ivy League university*."

Joni rolled her eyes and followed up with,

---

*Children don't need this pressure. They can and often are successful without a degree from an Ivy League...I mean I don't have one, and I think I'm doing well for myself.

"I don't want to go to HAAARVARD. I want to be a garbage truck driver."

Both Jules and Nic's heads lowered in defeat.

"Anything but a garbage truck driver!" They both undoubtedly thought.

Joni, Jules, and Nic's story is a textbook case of affluent parents pushing their children and not giving them enough downtime, all while believing this is the only path to success.

Stop me if you've heard this one before: a group of parents sitting around as their children participate in an activity. One parent mentions how busy their family is, and then…

The topping game is on!

The parents all try to convey why their family is the busiest.

It's exhausting!

But let me let you in on a little secret…it doesn't matter who is the busiest. The busiest family is not doing what's in the best interest of the parents, their children, or their families.

They're NOT winning! It's quite the opposite.

What's their opportunity cost for that busyness?

Family dinners.

Family vacations.

Laughter. Fun.

Real connection.

I can reassure you that when you're on your deathbed, you'll not regret not having your child participate in one more activity. But what you will regret is not spending more quality time with your family.

There's absolutely no need to schedule every second of your child's day. Allow time for unstructured time. This allows your child to exert some form of control over their lives.

If you don't want to relinquish some control over the schedule, then schedule every second of their day, don't let them have a sense of control. But trust, you will be in my office (or another mental health provider's), just like Joni, Jules, and Nic. And if they are in my office, then chances are they're meeting criteria for a psychological disorder, most likely one that stems from a feeling of a lack of control: obsessive compulsive disorder, anorexia, hoarding disorder, etc. Children develop these symptoms in an attempt to take some of the control back.

Believe me, I have enough parents who aren't reading this book, in my office paying my exorbitant fee[*]. So, save yourself some money. Twenty-nine bucks and ninety-nine cents is much better than $2000 (no, not an hour, I'm not that bougie, but probably how much you will spend on me addressing these issues) and allow your child some control.

Here's my favorite way to incorporate your child's wants and desires into the family schedule, the younger they are the better. I call it "The Plan for the Day."

Choose a time and place. Decide when and where your family will construct the plan for the day. Bedtime? Breakfast?

---

[*]It really isn't that high, but to me, growing up low income, my hourly fee seems like I'm a millionaire.

After dinner? I'd encourage you to pair it with something that is routine in your household. It's called habit stacking (Thanks, James Clear, author of *Atomic Habits*!). You're more likely to remember to do it (half the battle, am I right?) if it's paired with something you already routinely do. My family is an after-breakfast kind of family.

List out all tasks. Create a list together of tasks that you and your child need AND want to complete in the day. Don't skimp on communicating responsibilities, aka chores, that you expect your child to complete. Again, we don't want to sentence them to a life in our basements. But be sure there is a fair amount of downtime for both you and them.

I typically do this the previous night with my children, as I tuck them into their beds. I ask, "Is there anything you would like to do tomorrow?"

Construct the plan for the day. Rough outline!

It should NOT look like this:

9:00am-1:00pm: Volunteer at VBS

1:00pm: VBS Wrap up

2:28pm: Paint nails in car

2:30pm: Coffee with friend

3:30pm: Pick up girls from camp

3:35pm: Work phone call 1

3:41pm: Work phone call 2

3:48pm: Work phone call 3

4:00pm: Wine tasting

4:45pm: Drop off Daughter 1 for sleepover

5:00pm: Meet Daughter 2's friend for sleep under for dinner

5:57pm: Pet store with Daughter 2 and friend

6:12:27pm: Bathroom Break

6:15pm: Sleep under movie

8:30pm: Drop off sleep under friend

8:45pm: Swing by sleep over

9:30pm: Transition living room into camping to be unique for Daughter 2 because she didn't get a sleep over

This strategy of having a list of tasks to complete in a day is what a lot of newer time management strategists and businesses are moving towards. It allows for more life-work balance.

During construction, show them that they have a say. They have control. Not complete control, but some. Schedule in blocks of free time—allowing them time and space to explore and figure out how to spend their free time—what activities and games bring them joy.

Execute. You and your child complete the tasks for the day, check 'em off, and when you've completed them, then you're done! Go and live your life.

This is time for family rejuvenation. Please stop thinking about work. Practice some mindfulness and be completely present with your child and your partner.

Here's a recap of the four steps for creating "The Plan for the Day":

 Choose a time and place.

 List out all tasks.

 Construct the plan for the day.

 Execute.

And GREAT NEWS! Jules and Nic eventually, after months of sessions, convinced Joni to at least consider tennis classes, under one condition—they'd allow her more downtime throughout the day. She agreed to do tennis classes after she saw that tennis classes weren't going to be completely structured and planned as she originally thought. And they gave her some flexibility and enjoyment that she had been desiring, in addition to the more downtime throughout the day that she negotiated for.

I consider Joni, Jules, and Nic a partial therapy success story. Joni completed the therapeutic goals we had set out to accomplish. However, I have a feeling Jules and Nic will always keep a hyper busy schedule. It's like that old adage: you can take the parents out of the hyper busy city, but you can't take the hyper busy city out of the parents.

BONUS TIP: When your child is younger than middle school, I strongly recommend limiting the number of extracurricular activities to one at a time.

Yes, one.

I have research to support this, but I promised I wouldn't bore you with all of that. You're gonna have to trust me on this one.

HIGH EXPECTATIONS

TAMING TEMPER TANTRUMS

Cody, a thirty-something year old father with not one but three baby mamas, walked into my office, sat on the far-left side of the gray couch, and placed his 24 oz. bottle of Mountain Dew on the side table.

I enjoyed working with Cody because he possessed strong opinions that contradicted my own. I frequently pushed his buttons. And I laughed when he'd start sessions with, "You were right... ." I'd give him my self-righteous look, to which he would respond by telling me to "SHUT UP*."

I waited for him to start.

> "I need help parenting Hudson [7-year-old]."

> "What makes you think you're struggling with Hudson?"

> "Because, you'll not believe what he said to me."

I moved to the end of my seat because I knew this was going to be good because Cody's not one for hyperbole.

I asked,

> "What did he say?"

> "Oh, just you wait. I've gotta give you context."

I nodded, sat back, and, in my head, grabbed some popcorn.

> "On Saturday, Hudson and I woke up early so that he and I could go horseback riding together. Hudson had been bragging for weeks that he was better at horseback riding than me.

---

*How rude! Right? I didn't even say anything!

> And I thought, 'Well, no shit. I pay for you to ride every other week. I NEVER pay for myself to ride.'"

My head dropped immediately. I looked up and made eye contact and asked in almost a whisper,

> "You didn't say that...did you?"

> "No, but I thought it!"

> "Okay, good. At least some of the stuff I've taught you has sunk in."

I shot him my best self-righteous look.

> "Yeah, okay, doc. Anyway, we arrived at the barn and did all the things we needed to get the horses ready. Hudson jawed the whole time that he was going to show me how it was done. I put up with it for a little while, but then I dropped the hammer!"

> "Oh no."

> "I told him, 'Whatever you can do, I can do better, boy!'"

I closed my eyes for a few seconds, mustering all of my clinical skills, opened my eyes, and asked Cody,

> "What happened next?"

> "I showed him I was better at riding a horse than he was. I schooled his little, ungrateful ass! I couldn't walk the next day... but that's beside the point."

Cody shot me his cockiest smile.

> "I see that you're very proud of yourself, ass. Now, I'm guessing more happened than this..."

> "Yeah, we groomed the horses and grabbed some lunch at

> Chick-fil-A. He refused to eat all that much because he was still salty from me schooling him and then we didn't go where he wanted for lunch. Immediately after lunch, we headed to the storage unit to move my stuff to a larger one."

I put up my hands—signaling Cody to pause.

> "You mean to tell me, y'all went horseback riding, where you ridiculed him, you didn't let him choose where to have lunch, and THEN you forced him to move boxes??"

Cody nodded.

> I followed with, *"Just what a 7-year-old boy wants to do"* somewhat under my breath.

> "I'm not going to win a parenting award, am I?"

I mouthed *"No"* as I shook my head, followed by a smile and a hand gesture, encouraging Cody to continue with this train-wreck of a story.

> "After some time, Hudson started complaining, whining, and repeatedly asking, 'When are we going?' in that super whiny 7-year-old voice. And you know that sends shivers down my spine. At first, I ignored his question, but then after the 50th time, I told him we had a few more boxes to move then we'd be on our way. And you know what the little shit said to me?"

> "I can only imagine."

> "He looked up at me, with nothing but hate in his eyes, and said, 'I'm going to kill you.'"

As Cody finished his sentence, I responded in the way that any good clinical child psychologist would—I belly-laughed. Yes, straight belly-laughed. Believe me, I know! I am not the right fit for every client. What therapist laughs when a client's son says they're going to kill them? Me!

But come on. Kids say the funniest shit. AND Cody had it coming. We can all agree on that, right?!

Children throw temper tantrums because their bodies and minds are not in a homeostatic state.

A what?!

I know, I know, I promised in the intro that I wouldn't use big words, but homeostasis is a HUGE word for understanding why kids throw temper tantrums. Our bodies crave to be in a homeostatic state—meaning we like to be in the middle of the road for everything. We don't like to be too cold or too hot, hungry or overly full, too tired or get too much sleep, bored or overstimulated. We function best when our bodies and minds are right in the middle—the sweet spot.

And if we keep that in mind, then we can figure out why Hudson and all children throw temper tantrums:

- ☐ They're bored OR overstimulated

- ☐ They're experiencing big emotions such as anxiety OR feeling trapped/controlled

- ☐ They're tired OR need to move

- ☐ They're hungry/dehydrated OR have over-indulged

- ☐ They're experiencing disengagement OR over engagement

Thinking back to Cody and Hudson's story: which of these five was Hudson experiencing?

If you answered the first four, you could have my job.

No wonder he behaved in a way that was less than ideal.

Now, you might be sitting there thinking, "Did Hudson really have a temper tantrum? I mean, he just threatened his father's life...no biggie. If you want a story on temper tantrums, I could share a few...or hundreds."

That's the thing about temper tantrums—they come in all shapes and sizes. No two kids' tantrums are the same. One child's whine is another child's punching a hole in their bedroom wall and another's going limp in the middle of the grocery store—all examples of temper tantrums*.

And given the wide range of behaviors that fall under the category of "temper tantrum," every single child will throw their fair share. And if that's the case, then how do we treat them?

We don't.

I mean, yes, in the following chapters, I will share with you all the strategies I use with my own children and clients' children to navigate temper tantrums, but the best way to "treat" temper tantrums is to prevent them.

You've just read why children (and adults) throw temper tantrums, so let's cover practical ways to prevent them from ever happening.

---

*I once heard an influencer brag that his daughter NEVER had a temper tantrum. MALARKEY! There ain't no way! Not because he wasn't a great dad, I mean, I don't know him personally, but given his principle of positive parenting, I would hope he is at least a good dad. That would be like me being a terrible mother...

When your child throws a temper tantrum:

 Use the skills you developed by reading "Adapt!"

 Decipher which cause or causes is/are the most likely culprit(s)

 Use the practical solutions provided below:

BORED: Sing songs. Play I spy. Carry books, activity books, crayons, and markers with you. Yes, you could always hand them your phone or a tablet, but there's something to be said about classic ways of entertaining our child—they stimulate the brain. Your child is bored! Activate their brain by having them read or get creative. Don't shut off their brains.

OVERSTIMULATED: Quiet time. Try to reduce the amount of stimulation: sounds, sights, physical senses. Give them a few moments to simply be.

FEEL ANXIOUS: Children can be anxious for a variety of reasons like their bodies are anxious, they don't know what is expected of them, or they're in a new environment.

If your child's body is anxious, I always like trying to make physical contact first when I see they're anxious. Hug them. Hold their hand. Bring them into your lap*. Encourage them to breathe.

For the other two reasons given, read "Adapt!"

FEEL TRAPPED/CONTROLLED: Schedule time for them to do what they or their bodies want to do. Cough, cough—let them choose lunch.

TIRED: When scheduling events, allocate time for naps and/

---

*Age appropriate, please! And make sure they're OK with this gesture.
I don't foresee a 12 yo boy wanting this in his life.

or quiet time. Yes, I realize it's a pain in the ass to stop what you're doing to allow your child to nap or have quiet time, but if your child needs it so that they don't throw a colossal tantrum in the middle of the grocery store, isn't your sanity, ego, and well-being worth that?

NEED TO MOVE: Walk places. Park farther out. Dance. Shake your tushies. Get the giggles out. Take regular movement breaks.

HUNGRY: Always have snacks on hand. Think glovebox, pockets, and your purse/bag/diaper bag.

DEHYDRATED: Have refillable water bottles, always. Pack portable milk, juice, or Kool-Aid.

OVER INDULGED: Portion control. Food guidelines. Keep consistent (Re-read, Consistency, Consistency, Consistency).

DISENGAGED: A lot of time when we are on the move, we can get caught up in all the things we need to do, and we forget that our children need to be connected to us. Check in with them occasionally. Strike up a conversation in the car. Buy "*Questions for Humans**.*"

OVER ENGAGED: Alone time or small group interactions. Similar to overstimulation.

I believe Cody turned a corner after this story. I mean, if one of my kids told me they were going to kill me, I think it would be about time to reflect on my parenting. Now, when Cody comes in for the occasional session, it's clear that Hudson's homeostatic state is kept in mind when they come up with the plan for the day.

---

*My dear friend, Dr. John Delony, created these stack of cards with thought-provoking questions on them. He has one specifically for parents.

WHY KIDS DO WHAT THEY DO

Mindy, a 12-year-old girl, sat in my office totally defeated, wearing a Monkey D. Luffy anime shirt and picked at her black nail polish.

> "Mindy, based on the data I've collected over the last 30 days, you have threatened to kill yourself 29 of those days. Please tell me about the rock incident the other day outside the field house."
>
> "Well, you know how cute I think Danny is and I was finally getting the chance to talk to him. We were totally bonding over our combined love of anime, but then Morgan walked by, and Danny dropped me and followed her like a little puppy."
>
> "What feeling surged when Danny acted like Doug the Pug?"
>
> "Rejected."
>
> "That must have been difficult. What happened next?"
>
> "I walked through Morgan and Danny's little love fest, bumped into Morgan, mean mugged her, and then ran out of the field house. Morgan didn't appreciate my actions and followed me. Danny acted like the good doggy he is and followed his master."
>
> "And?"
>
> "I grabbed the biggest rock I could find, used all my strength to pick it up, and held it over my head. I threatened to drop it unless Danny stopped talking to Morgan."
>
> "How'd that work out?"
>
> "Okay. I got to spend the rest of the evening with my favorite case worker, Beverley."

"And what about the cord incident?"

"HA! I was at the house. Tamra, Anna, and Betsy were blabbing about boys they're 'talking' to. I tried to join in, but they boxed me out, and told me to go away...So I did. But I didn't go far.

"I walked to the window, pulled the blinds all the way up, and wrapped the cord around my neck a few times and started pulling it up and tighter. Tamra and Anna ran to me and wrestled the cord out of my hands and Betsy got Jeremy."

"Oh. Okay. What feeling did you experience when they wouldn't include you?"

"Rejected."

"And how'd wrapping the cord around your neck work out for ya?"

"Meh. I got to spend a few hours with Beverley by myself."

"And lastly, talk to me about the butcher knife incident?"

"It was my turn to help Jeremy and Gwen with dinner. They were telling me the story about how they met and it's the cutest story like ever. But then it triggered me to think how my mum abandoned me and left me on the streets in India to fend for myself. I was overcome by all the flashbacks. I just wanted them to stop. I grabbed the butcher knife and put it to my chest."

"That sounds rough! I'm sorry the flashbacks hit so hard. What feeling accompanied them?"

"Rejection."

"And what happened immediately after Gwen got you to put the knife down?"

"Jeremy called Beverley and I got to spend the evening playing board games with her."

And at that moment, I found myself wondering an age-old question.

As parents we often find ourselves asking, "Why?"

Why does my child want yet another Squishmallow?

Why did my child call me an asshole?

Why does my child steal my phone and take multiple pictures of their poop?

There's a group of psychologists who believe all behaviors can be explained by one of four why's.

1. Attention: Pretty self-explanatory. It can be positive or negative attention--children are equal opportunity attention seekers! Attention is your child's currency. They will do anything to get more of it.

2. Escape/Avoidance: They're wanting to get out of a situation that makes them uncomfortable. This can also be negative emotions and feelings. Usually when I see people procrastinating or becoming easily distracted, it's because they are avoiding an uncomfortable situation or feeling.

3. Tangibles: They want something concrete. Think money, food, toys, electronics, extra video game time, etc.

4. Automatic Response: It feels good.

This is by far the most infuriating one for parents to grapple with because most parents don't see it as an explanation for behavior. It goes something like this:

Parent: "Why did you do that?"

Child: "Because I wanted to."

Parent: "That is not a reasonable explanation!"

Rinse and repeat until someone educates the parent that, "Because I wanted to or because it felt good," is, in fact, an explanation.

To figure out why your child does what she does, you'll need to collect some data. When your child does the specific behavior, write down what was going on immediately before and after she engaged in the behavior.

If you jump back up to Mindy's story, you'll notice that my questions are getting me the data that I needed to understand Mindy's why. The behavior I was trying to better understand was her suicidal behaviors. Mindy felt rejected immediately before she engaged in suicidal behavior, and Mindy got to spend time with Beverley after the suicidal behavior.

Once you have data, then you can figure out why your child is doing what they're doing.

Mindy engaged in suicidal behaviors because she was trying to escape feeling rejection and wanted attention. But she lacked both the coping skills to navigate the rejection and the relationship skills to ask for attention in a socially appropriate way.

Once you figure out why your child is doing what they're doing, then you can tailor how you respond. You're no longer giving them money (tangible) when all they want is quality time with you (attention). You stop spinning your wheels in the non-stop mental "why" hamster wheel.

What did this look like for Mindy? We incorporated coping, relationship building, and social skills into her treatment plan. And after we made that tweak, Mindy's suicidal threats went way down.

Now, yes, I know you have probably watched all the behavior analysis shows like *Criminal Minds*, and have listened to all the true crime podcasts, and think that you are a behavioral analyst. Easy, tiger.

Applying this skill and hence understanding why your child does what she does will take some time, practice, patience, and a whole lot of grace.

Here's a breakdown:

 Identify the behavior you want to better understand and change

 Collect data by writing down what happened immediately before and after your child did the behavior

 Look at the list of 4 why's and decide which one fits best

 Alter how you respond to fit why your child is doing what they're doing

Throughout this section of the book, with the exception of the last two parenting tips, you can practice figuring out why the child is behaving in the way they are.

After all, practice makes progress.

SEEING RED

Dennis [9 year old] and Alice (Dennis's mom) walked in and sat down. Dennis claimed one of the chairs while Alice sat on the couch. I noticed right away that Dennis really didn't want to be in therapy today and Alice sported a nasty scowl.

I started the session with my typical therapy opener, using a lighter and more playful tone given what I read on their faces and bodies,

"So, how's the week been?"

After an awkward (yet brief, thank goodness) pause, Dennis said,

"The babysitter quit."

"Does that make her the fifth or sixth babysitter who quit this year (mind you, it was April!)?"

Dennis dropped his head and replied,

"Seventh."

"Oh man. What happened?"

"Polly's (his older sister) birthday was a few days ago, and Mom filled the living room with balloons. Yesterday, while Mom worked, Georgette babysat us. Polly, Maggie (younger sister), and I were all playing nicely (Dennis shot Alice a look) in the living room, but instead of playing with us, Georgette messed around on her phone."

Alice sighed at Dennis's exasperated emphasis of his last phrase.

"Anyway. Georgette wasn't paying attention to us, so I started playing 'Lunatic*' with Polly and Maggie. And Dr. Andrea, you know how I get when I play Lunatic... ."

"Who did you make cry?"

"Polly."

"On her birthday?!"

"Her birthday was a few days ago..."

"Oh, so that isn't AS bad?"

"Nope! ANYWAY, Georgette didn't stop me because she was on her phone. I mean, goodness, she didn't even notice Polly crying! To make Polly laugh, I started grabbing as many balloons as I could. But there was a balloon that none of us could reach because the string was too short. I solved the problem like you taught me (Dennis shot me a grin) and climbed the entertainment center and reached for the balloon as I held on.

"Georgette saw me and yelled,
'DENNIS! GET DOWN FROM THERE RIGHT THIS INSTANT! YOU CAN FALL AND HURT YOURSELF! I DON'T WANT TO TEXT YOUR MOM AND TELL HER WE'RE GOING TO THE ER! AND WHAT A BAD EXAMPLE YOU'RE BEING FOR MAGGIE! SHE SEES YOU AND THEN SHE WANTS TO DO IT TOO!'"

After sharing, Dennis exhaustingly threw himself on the couch with Alice.

I paused to process the scene and gave Alice a minute to console Dennis.

---

*"Lunatic" is the family's game for the children acting silly, but Dennis ALWAYS takes it a little too far and becomes a little too aggressive. Therefore, the family doesn't play it very often.

"Okay, I understand you getting mad at Georgette for being on her phone, not playing with y'all, and then yelling at you for problem solving. Is that all to the story? I couldn't imagine Georgette would quit because of that... ."

"Go ahead, Dennis, tell Dr. Andrea, what you did next."

Dennis lifted his head from Alice's armpit, stared at her for a few seconds, covered his face with a pillow, and then muffled something.

"A what? I can't hear you. Well, because you have a pillow in front of your face."

With Alice's encouragement, Dennis lowered the pillow and then repeated himself,

"A knife."

"Ah. Tell me what made you grab a knife."

"I wanted to pop all of Polly's balloons."

"And a kitchen knife was the best way to do that?"

"Bad choice, huh?"

"Maybe just a little,"

I said, as I put a little space between my thumb and pointer finger, tilted my head, and shrugged my shoulders.

Dennis and Alice both giggled.

"Okay, but what did Georgette do when you came back to the living room holding a knife?"

75

"*Her face looked like this* (Dennis demonstrates a face that is a mix of scared and shocked), *and she yelled for Polly and Maggie to get behind her.*"

Alice interrupted Dennis and provided the following insight,

"*Georgette thought he was going to stab or cut one of them.*"

"*ALL I WANTED WAS TO POP THE BALLOONS! I didn't want to hurt Polly or Maggie.*"

"*I can see why Georgette would jump to the conclusion she did. What happened after she put your sisters behind her?*"

"*I yelled at Georgette and tried to tell her I just wanted to pop the balloons. But she wouldn't listen to me. I realized she wasn't hearing me, so I took the knife back to the kitchen.*"

Alice chimed in,

"*Georgette then texted me, asked me to come home right then and there, and as soon as I pulled into the driveway, Georgette stormed out the door and quit.*"

Dennis, Alice, and myself spent the rest of the session creating a behavior chain and analyzing it.

It looked like this:

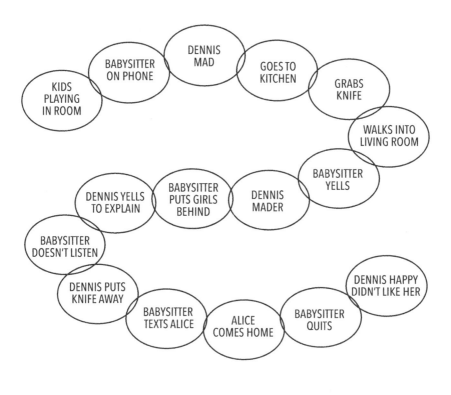

A behavior chain is a technique to better understand our child's behavior in a particular situation. Each behavior, thought, or emotion gets its own link, and you plot out the situation from start to finish. It helps to realize when someone sees red–they are angry beyond reason–and therefore, sees what their build up looks like. The goal is to figure out where the chain can be broken by someone making a different behavioral choice. This could be either the child or the parent. Given the interactional nature of relationships, it's rarely one person's fault for a situation going sideways.

Once we drew out the behavior chain, we could figure out why Dennis in his own words, "became a lunatic." Based off what you read in "Why Kids Do What They Do", which of the four functions (attention, escape/avoidance, tangibles, or automatic response) best explains Dennis's overall behavior?

Do do do do do do doo do do do do do do...*

BUZZ!

Did you guess attention?

Then you may be becoming a behavioral modification expert.

It's attention, because Dennis got mad when the babysitter was ignoring them by being on her phone. This is a recurring problem for Dennis. He goes from 0 to 60 when someone who's supposed to be taking care of him is on their phone instead of asking for attention in a socially appropriate way... you know, ways that don't involve knives.

Another benefit of a behavior chain is it allows us as parents to take responsibility for the role we played in things going sideways and learn how to parent more intentionally the next time. For example, in this scenario, where could the babysitter learn from her mistakes?

First, the babysitter was on her phone instead of actively playing with the children. She was so engrossed in her phone that she didn't recognize that the children couldn't reach the balloon. I mean, not to be super judgy, but c'mon! You can't see or hear three kids trying to reach balloons?! This situation could have been easily prevented had she simply been engaged with the children.

---

*Think *Jeopardy* theme song.

Second, the babysitter jumped to conclusions. Now, I won't judge her at all for this one. I get it. A little boy was coming at her and his siblings with a knife! Talk about your fight, flight, or freeze system being activated. I'm pretty sure most parents —not counting the badass parents in the military or law enforcement who have been trained to stay cool, calm, and collected when someone is coming at them with a knife— would respond similarly.

But if we are learning from our mistakes as parents, then we want to activate your and the child's logical portions of your brains by practicing:

 Staying cool, calm, and collected
(See Cool as a Cucumber)

 Make an observational statement such as, "I see you have a knife."

 Then follow it up with a question, "What do you plan to do with that knife?"

I love me some behavior chains. I use them (to some of my clients' dismay) all the time in therapy. They are helpful in all areas of life, not just parenting. I recommend first writing them out, but once you've practiced with them enough, you can accomplish them mentally.

Alice opted to drop down to part-time work and therefore the family no longer relies as heavily on babysitters. And when they do need a babysitter, they typically use babysitters who understand Dennis and his behaviors really well and know not to be on their phones when babysitting for the Mitchell's.

COOL AS A CUCUMBER

"What brings you in?"

I asked Kate, as her four-year-old son, JJ, played in the corner—positioned in a way to keep an eye on me.

"JJ is getting in trouble at daycare, and they're about to kick him out."

"What is he doing that's getting him in trouble?"

"DON'T ANSWER THAT, YOU BITCH!"

Kate shot me a helpless look, and I stepped in.

"Hey JJ! Thanks for contributing. Would you like to answer my question?"

"I'm not saying anything to you!"

JJ scowled.

"Oh, okay. Well, mom and I are going to talk. You keep playing and let me know if you want to say something."

JJ went back to playing, still glancing at me.

"So Kate, what behaviors is JJ doing that's getting him in trouble?"

Kate glanced at JJ, and then back to me.

"He's swearing, kicking, pushing, and punching other children when he gets upset."

"I'M GOING TO CUT YOU!"

Before Kate looked at JJ, I grabbed her attention.

Kate brought her attention back to me.

"We're going to chat and ignore any potty mouth language. How does that sound?"

Kate meekly nodded.

"Okay, when did JJ start behaving this way?"

"About five months ago."

"Okay, did anything happen five months ago."

"Yes, his father..."

"SHUT THE FUCK UP!"

"Hey, JJ. What is your daddy's name?

"Tom."

"Thank you."

JJ continued playing.

"Kate, what is your relationship status with Tom?"

"We've been married for five years."

"Okay. And what is your relationship like with Tom?"

JJ glared at his mom and waited for a response.

"We were doing good for many years, but then five months ago..."

"Hey Kate, you can say what you need to say. If JJ reacts aggressively, we will simply ignore him and continue chatting."

I waited for her agreement.

"Could JJ have learned some of the behaviors getting him in trouble from home about five months ago?"

"Yes."

"And if this behavior has been going on for five months, why seek services now?"

"Because they've worsened and they're going to kick him out."

"Oh. Okay. Did something happen around the time that it worsened?"

"STOP ASKING QUESTIONS, BITCH!"

"Tom pushed me and hit me. I've had enough. I decided to leave him a few days ago..."

"I WILL KILL YOU, YOU BITCH!"

I motioned to grab Kate's attention and quickly said,

"What else were you going to say, Kate?"

"JJ and I are staying at my sister's house. I'm gonna get a restraining order against Tom. And JJ is not happy about it."

"I'm going to stab you when you're sleeping and run away with Daddy."

The rest of our initial session played out in a similar manner. The only difference was I was the one who experienced the brunt of JJ's anger: he saw me as a person who was going to help his mother leave his father.

Kate and JJ returned for the next session, and to my surprise, with Tom. It turns out, Kate didn't want to leave Tom—

she simply wanted the relationship to improve. Throughout the session, it was apparent that JJ was still convinced that I was trying to encourage Kate to leave Tom, which wasn't my intent*.

JJ tried to distract us, and he knew from the initial session that using profanities wouldn't get him the reaction he wanted. So, JJ grabbed the shiniest thing in the room, a glass lava globe, and dropped it—shattering it. And so my 90's lava lamp obsession is now no more.

As soon as it hit the floor, JJ looked at me.

I frowned slightly and immediately turned my attention to Tom. In the calmest voice I could muster, I explained,

> "We are going to stay cool, calm, and collected."

Tom looked at me as if I was absolutely nuts.

He reacted with,

> "We aren't going to yell at him? Spank him? Reprimand him?"

I responded with,

> "Again, we are going to stay cool, calm, and collected. It's only a material item. We are going to reprimand him, but differently. We aren't going to yell or spank him because that's how he expects us to react. See, he did what he did because he wanted the attention away from the two of you."

I paused and allowed Kate and Tom to acknowledge what I had said and turned my attention to JJ.

---

*My goal isn't to break up families, but to help them function better, whether that is by teaching individual coping skills, relationship skills, or parenting skills. But if it seems like a family is too far gone, I'll help them make that transition less disruptive for all parties.

I walked over to JJ, squatted down, and made eye contact.

> "That was not cool, and, as a consequence, you'll help me clean it up."

I picked up the pieces of glass and threw them in the trash. I gave him a roll of paper towels.

> "Now I expect you to use these and dry up the liquid like this."

I showed him how and then he mimicked the behavior without question.

> "That is good cleaning up, JJ. Please continue cleaning everything up."

I returned to my chair and turned to Kate and Tom.

> "Did you see what I did there? How's my reaction different than how you would've reacted?"

Tom spoke immediately and said,

> "I would've shouted at him and spanked him."

> "Hmmm...and how's that working for you? How would he have behaved?"

Kate and Tom looked at each other.

Kate stated,

> "He would have laughed. Or yelled back. Or ran away."

> "You saw how he responded to my instruction. Would you prefer his typical response or the way he responded to me?"

Very sheepishly, Tom responded,

> "How he was with you."

"Ah. Hmm. So, are you interested in learning how I did that?"

"Sure."

We can't react to a child's undesirable behavior—behavior that grinds your gears—in a way they expect. If you do, they win! And I don't know about you, but I'm a competitive person, and I don't want my child winning when they're behaving in a way that I don't want them to. The default is modeling good emotion regulation and staying cool, calm, and collected.

Good emotion regulation sets our child up for success. I've seen way too many folks lose everything because they were in an emotional mind and flew off the handle. I once heard on a podcast that a high percentage of convicted murderers who are in prison wish they could have those 5 minutes back where they took another person's life.

Nothing good comes from acting while in emotional mind. Last time I checked, unless we are all replaced by robots—Terminator-style—humans are going to experience emotions. They aren't going away. So, we might as well learn good emotional regulation skills and model them for our child.

More is caught than taught.

My favorite emotional regulation skill: Opposite Action.

It's exactly how it sounds—you do the complete opposite behavior of how you are feeling.

If you want to yell, whisper.

If you want to throw something, you ever so gently place it down.

If you want to kick or punch someone, hug them.

Opposite action is anything but easy. It takes a lot of practice; but, once you can master this coping skill, you're sitting pretty, not just in parenting, but in life.

Here are the steps for opposite action:

 Pause

 Close your eyes

 Pull your shoulders away from your ears

 Inhale through your nose for 5 seconds

 Hold your breath for 2 seconds

 Exhale from your mouth for 8 seconds.

 Ask yourself what behavior your emotion is telling you to do right now

 Do the opposite

99.9% of the time (I made this stat up, and I don't even know what that .1% of the time would look like), opposite action requires you to be as cool as a cucumber, calm, and collected.

I also love opposite action because it freaks people the heck out! They're expecting you to yell and then you come in whispering. It's unsettling. It stops them in their tracks. And that pause gives you the opportunity you need to modify their behavior.

Unfortunately, Kate, Tom and JJ stopped coming to therapy after session two. My guess is the parenting behaviors I suggested were too foreign to both Kate and Tom. They were too far outside what they viewed as "normal" parenting.

And this may also be the case for you, but I ask you, "Is what you're currently doing as a parent working for you?" If the answer to that question is a resounding, "NO!" Then why not give what I'm suggesting a try?

CATCH AND IGNORE

Diane looked at me as if I had eight heads—Medusa style—during our first therapy session, no doubt questioning her decision of staying with the rookie therapist a week ago during the initial session. Diane was the grandmother to Adrianne [4 year old] and Joey [2 year old]. She had full custody of her grandchildren because their mother was addicted to drugs and would prostitute herself out while her children were in the apartment and sometimes even in the same room*.

> *"Let me get this straight, Andrea...You want me to praise Adrianne and Joey when I catch them doing something I want them to do more of, and ignore anything that they're doing or saying that I want them to do less of, as long as they aren't harming themselves or others?"*

> *"Yes, praise the hell out of them when they're doing a behavior that warms your heart. Be as specific as you can be with what behavior you want to reinforce. Say something like, 'OH Joey! I really like how quietly and appropriately you're playing with those Barbies.'"*

> *"Ahhh, ha."*

I gave Diane a reassuring smile and continued.

> *"AND don't forget! Ignore any and all behaviors that grind your gears, unless they are hurting you or each other. If they do or say anything inappropriate, look the other way, no matter what it is."*

---

*After you read that, if you had the thought, "MAN! I have never done that! I'm doing pretty well," Yes. Yes, you would be correct. If you have never done something this traumatizing in front of your child, then you're doing pretty okay as an intentional parent, but do you really want this to be the bar that you set???? No? I didn't think so. Keep reading!

> "Okay...and that's ALL you want me to do this whole week."
>
> "Yep. I know it sounds gimmicky and like it's not going to work, but I'm gonna need you to trust me, just like you did during the initial session when you told me you wanted to stay with me instead of going with a more experienced therapist."

I paused and gave Diane a minute because she looked like she was working through something—realizing something.

Diane went to say something, but then stopped.

> "Go ahead, what is it?"
>
> "Is that why you didn't say anything to Joey when he said... you know...when the boy Barbie asked the girl Barbie... that question?"

I laugh ever so gently, relieving some of the tension in the air, remembering that initial session and just how few boundaries Adrianne and Joey possessed due to what they had witnessed and experienced living with their mother.

> "Yes. And what happened when we ignored how he was playing, because he was playing quietly, inappropriately yes, but still he wasn't hurting himself or anyone else?"
>
> "He only had the boy Barbie ask once and then moved on to playin' how kids should play with Barbies."
>
> "Exactly. So will you try it out? Just for a week. If you come back next week and tell me, 'Andrea, that most definitely didn't work,' we'll change it up or I'll find you the best therapist in this place."

Diane's face lit up, smiled, and she low key shouted,

> "DEAL!"

Think about what behaviors you want to see your child do more of? What behaviors do you want to see your child do less of? Chances are you don't have to think very hard, because you probably have a visceral reaction to these behaviors.

When you see your child do something and it warms your heart, well, then you want to see more of this behavior. When you see your child do something and it grinds your gears, well, then you want to see less of this behavior.

Ask yourself, "Does this behavior warm my heart or grind my gears?" If it warms your heart, praise them. Acknowledge what they're doing. Stop, drop whatever it is that you are doing, and tell your child how much you appreciate whatever behavior they are currently doing. But it should be specific, concrete, and immediate.

For example, "Buddy, I love how you shared your toy with your sister. Thank you so much!"

Compared to "Hey, kid. Great job."

See the difference? In the first one, the child now knows exactly what behavior they need to exhibit to earn praise. They can replicate it.

In the second one, they're left guessing. And maybe, they were thinking about and doing something they weren't supposed to be doing (i.e., picking their nose and wiping the boogers on your SUV door), but by you telling them "Great job." they will replicate that behavior because you gave them nondescript praise.

The more outrageously positive, the better.

We want to create a contrast to the second half of this tip—ignore all behaviors that you want to see less of.

If the behavior grinds your gears, I want you to completely ignore the behavior. Go into a different room. Say nothing. Continue doing whatever it was that you were doing.

This is not easy. Believe me. You will need to manage your own reactions, because sometimes we react when we didn't mean to or realize it. Your facial expressions count as reacting and responding. If your child sees that they have your number, they win. Don't let them win! And you don't let them win by walking out of the room or distracting yourself by doing something else.

But here is the trick and once you can tackle this, you're going to start to see real changes. As soon as your child changes from a behavior that grinds your gears to a behavior that warms your heart, praise the hell out of them!

Acknowledge!

Reinforce!

This is the contrast that makes big changes happen.

They'll see what behaviors gain them attention versus what behaviors get them ignored, something that no child wants.

 Ask yourself, "Does this behavior warm my heart or grind my gears?"

 Praise specifically, concretely, and immediately if it warms your heart.

 Ignore if it grinds your gears and it isn't hurting anyone.

And if you're like the grandmother and are sitting there on your porcelain throne doubting me and questioning why the hell you bought this book, all I ask is that you try it for one week. One week and see what happens.

I'll sit here and wait for the emails, messages, and social media posts tagging me (@drdremata) shouting my praises. See what I just did there??? I promise, I'm a humble and modest person, not an egotistical maniac. I am simply confident in effective, science-based parenting practices communicated in ways that people can actually understand and implement.

It worked for Diane. She came back a week later and was completely floored. She was over the moon. She came in with such a bounce in her step. She could not wait to tell me how much catching them being good and ignoring the vast majority of bad behavior worked for her and her grandchildren. She raved about how good they were, especially in the grocery store. She told me she would never doubt me again. And she didn't.

I eventually transferred Diane and her grandchildren to the next intern from the same school I attended. That intern would regularly update me on how well Diane and her grandchildren were doing—Diane turned into the ideal client.

POSITIVE REINFORCEMENT, YOUR FIRST LINE OF DEFENSE

When the twins were four and Chloe was two, Jim and I wanted our children to dress themselves. You know, develop some autonomy. Life skills. The basics! And I did what any good clinical child psychologist does—bribed them. Wait! I mean... I reinforced them.

I explained early one morning that for every article of clothing they put on by themselves, they would earn one whole M&M.

Yes, one M&M.

We're stingy with sweets. Hence, why none of our children have had any cavities.

Charlotte sauntered out of her bedroom, towards me, wearing jeans over shorts, a tank top over a long-sleeved shirt, with a sweatshirt on top of all of that, and not one, but two socks on each of her feet.

My mouth fell open as Charlotte counted,

"*1, 2, 3, 4, 5, 6, 7, 8, 9 M&M's please, Mama!*"

I squatted and got down to Charlotte's eye level, wrapped my arm around her waist and said,

"*Mija (a Spanish term of endearment meaning my daughter), I'm so happy that you put all these clothes on by yourself. Thank you. And you will earn the nine M&Ms this time, but from now on, you will only earn a M&M for each piece of clothing that is appropriate and reasonable. Do you understand?"*

Charlotte, with a smirk (because she knew she gamed me), nodded her head and said,

"Yes, Mama."

See. I'm not the perfect parent and I hope you love this story as much as I do.

The big takeaway from my parenting fail is, I praised the desired behavior (Charlotte putting on her clothes), while shaping* the undesirable interpretation.

And now I want to go all Mythbusters on "bribing" your kid.

MYTH 1: Rewards need to be lavish to work.

Truth: As I demonstrated, kids will work for very little. It's us parents and society (hello $30,000 birthday party for a four-year-old) who are always thinking we need to give more.

NOPE!

Start with the least amount of reward to get them to do the behavior. Now with that said, it must be enticing enough. For example, my mother-in-law tried to get my husband to make his bed every day by giving him a dollar if he made his bed every day for a week. Jim didn't think the dollar was worth the effort, so yeah, our bed is never made.

Rewards don't even need to cost anything.

---

*You'll learn about this in the next parenting tip.

Here is a list of some of my favorite no cost rewards:

 Quality time   Screen time

 Video game time   A trip to the park

 A hike   Bike rides

 A ride on Sandy the Horse from Meijer (yeah, yeah, it costs a penny)

MYTH 2: Rewards make kids "reward-hungry creatures" who will only do things if they receive a reward for doing it.

Truth: This may happen temporarily, but we can work with it. I find giving rewards immediately after the child does the behavior and every time the child does the behavior is effective at the beginning.

How do you train a dog?

You give them a treat after every time they do the trick, dontcha? Training a child to do behaviors they don't readily want to do is no different.

Once it becomes more of a habit, you start reinforcing more randomly. Then they will continue to do the behavior because they don't know when the reward is coming. This is the reward schedule that slot machines use to hook folks.

Another strategy for delaying the reward is requiring them to do the behavior X number of times before they get a bigger reward.

For example, if my children want to go to a trampoline park and I want them to clean the house, I will print off a sign for the trampoline park.

I will cut the sign up into 12 pieces and give them one piece for every 15 minutes that they clean*. Once they get all 12 pieces, then trampoline park here we come!

MYTH 3: Rewards work for all behaviors.

Truth: Rewards work best for tedious, boring, mindless, behaviors that no one really wants to do. Think cleaning, taking showers, walking the dog, brushing teeth, doing homework, changing the cat litter, exercising, eating healthy, etc.

We don't want to reward behaviors that our children find joy in—behaviors they are internally motivated to do. Giving them a reward for something they already readily do and enjoy is going to kill the joy.

Don't kill their joy!

For example, do not offer to pay your very studious child $20 for every A they earn on their report card. It will rob them of their joy of learning, and it will break your bank. No one wants either of those two things.

Now, if you have a child who hates school, finds it BORING, and struggles hardcore academically, then by all means offer that child money for higher grades.

Remember the parenting tip, "One Size Doesn't Fit All." Kids will be reinforced by different things.

---

*Pro Tip: You'll most likely need to remind them to clean up. Try something like this, "Hey kiddos, after dinner we'll do 15 minutes of clean-up so that y'all earn a trampoline park piece for today."

Here are some other rewards:

- food (sweets, favorites)
- toys
- stickers
- shoes
- pets
- art supplies
- amusement parks
- money
- outings/dates
- clothing
- tickets
- accessories
- instruments

It's up to you as the parent to figure out what works for your specific child.

Reinforcement is the best way to modify behavior—bar none. Anyone who thinks punishment is the way to go, evidently never thought about why the vast majority of Americans go to work: not because they listen to or read Ken Coleman's *From Paycheck to Purpose* and have found their calling, but because they get paid. Money, money, mon-ey, MONEY!

Use rewards whenever you want to see more of a behavior. Think of the behaviors your child does that warm your heart and then give them something they want after they do it.

This works on kids, your significant other, dogs, pretty much any mammal. Some have said, not cats, though, but I have yet to test this hypothesis...I'm not at cat person.

Figure out what specific behavior you want to see more of and then what is the person willing to work for.

Here are the positive reinforcement steps:

 Decide what behavior you want your child to do more

 Ask yourself whether the behavior is tedious, boring or mindless? (see Myth 3).

 Choose a reward that is worth your child's effort (see Myth 1)

 Explicitly tell your child about the reward and describe what behavior they need to do to earn the reward

---

Two years later and our three children still work for very little. Their preferred reward has moved from predominantly food rewards to screen time. It's amazing what we can get them to do (i.e., clean a whole room) for 10 minutes of PBS app time.

OH, NO! You cleaned a room, now you're practicing reading and math in a fun way, and Jim and I get 30 minutes of reduced noise in our house.

That's just terrible.

<Insert Dr. Dre's evil laugh>

TREAT YOUR CHILD'S BEHAVIOR LIKE PLAY-DOH

"Andrea, your client has arrived."

My textbox popped up notifying me that it's "go" time with a family. I put my therapist face on and walked down the hall to the waiting room.

"Well, hello, DunBrochs!"

I announced my arrival to the waiting room with my booming voice.

Mrs. Elinor DunBroch, her oldest son, Hamish, and her younger son, Hubert, acknowledged my presence with reciprocal boisterous responses, *"Hey!"*

Then came the whispered voice of a 8 year old, "Hello, Miss Andrea" from the middle child*, Merida.

I ignored her and continued to engage Elinor, Hamish, and Hubert in conversation.

"Hello, Miss Andrea"

said Merida, in a slightly raised voice, but not enough of an increase for me to reinforce the behavior, yet. I ignored it, and continued to ask Hamish about the newest information he had learned about space.

"HELLO, MISS ANDREA!"

"NOW THAT'S WHAT I'M TALKING ABOUT, MERIDA! HIGH FIVE!"

---

*Stop it! I know what you're thinking, "Of course, it's the middle child!" Nope! There is no research to support the middle child gets screwed. More unsupported pop psychology that needs to be stopped!

Merida gave me a high five and together we headed to the therapy room, talking about what she wanted to talk about.

"So, Merida. How are you doing today?"

"I'm doing good. My mommy got me a new dolly today, do you want to see it?"

"Absolutely!"

We arrived at the therapy room, just the two of us; all my focus was on Merida for the next 30 minutes. She earned her admittance to the therapy room, where she got all my attention and didn't have to share with her older brother, Hamish (who demands a lot of attention due to some of his more aggressive past behaviors) or with her younger brother, Hubert, who naturally commands attention with his larger-than-life personality.

If you are sitting there, on your porcelain throne thinking that I'm a huge B-I-T-C-H, I can see where you're coming from.

But please know, this was not my intent. The method that I used with Merida is called "shaping." The textbook definition of shaping is reinforcing approximations for the desired behavior.

Say what?!

In English: You give the child something they want when they engage in a behavior that is even slightly closer to the behavior that you are trying to get them to do—the behavior that is going to warm your heart.

Merida originally came to me because Elinor decided that she did not like how Merida didn't have a "voice." Meaning, she didn't like how soft-spoken and meek her daughter was. Elinor is a highly-educated woman who voluntarily resigned from her career to take care of Hamish and the special needs required of a child who has been diagnosed with Asperger's Disorder.

Merida, in Elinor's image, was a blob of white Play-Doh and she wanted me to help Merida develop her voice-molding Merida into one of those beautifully creative multi-colored Play-Doh structures* that some moms have the artistic ability to do.

I opted for shaping. I only paid attention to Merida when she would use a voice volume that was consistent with expectations.

Now, that is not where we started from—that's not how shaping works. We started by figuring out what is the baseline of the behavior: what volume does Merida typically use. Then, I set the bar a little bit higher, increased the metaphorical volume knob a line higher. Then I would only pay attention to her, throughout our sessions when we were alone together, when she spoke at this level. Then, the next week, the bar would be a little bit higher and so forth.

This specific shaping technique focuses on increasing or decreasing a behavior, where you give a reinforcer for either increasing the time or volume or decreasing the time or volume of a specific behavior.

---

*I don't like mixing Play-Doh colors and therefore have never created one of these. I also don't have an artistic bone in my body. My bestie and graphic designer on this book creates some of the best Play-Doh structures you've ever seen. I'm so jealous of her artistic ability.

Here are some other behaviors that are nicely modified using the same shaping technique I used with Merida:

  Increasing the amount of time your child... independently plays, stays with the same task, reads quietly, sits still

  Altering the volume your child speaks at

Now there are a slew of other behaviors that we want our children to do, but they're not inherent—meaning we didn't come out of our mother's womb knowing how to do these behaviors and they need to be learned:

  Ordering their own food and drinks

  Writing

  Sleeping by themselves in their own room

  Putting things away

  Cleaning specific rooms

  Feeding themselves

  Coloring within the lines

  Using the bathroom

  Tying shoes

  Brushing teeth

Here are the steps to use shaping to help your child learn these multiple step behaviors without you losing your mind:

 Choose a specific behavior

 Clearly identify all the steps that go into your child successfully carrying out that specific behavior

 Reinforce your child immediately after they hit the next step without assistance or prompting

 Raise the expectation to the succeeding step the next time and DO NOT reinforce for the previous expectation

With a little bit of shaping, you can mold your children into creative multi-colored Play-Doh sculptures.

After a few sessions, Merida was consistently using a "BIG voice," which got Merida the attention she craved and made Elinor extremely happy. Gone were the days when Hamish would choke out Merida because she would stay silent—white blob of Play-Doh behavior. Welcome the days when Merida was more confident, had a better sense of who she was, and almost always used her "BIG voice"—creative multi-colored Play-Doh structure behavior.

TELL. DON'T ASK.

Lightening Round!

Julianna, 3-year-old girl:

"Nice job pooping! Can you flush the toilet?"

"No."

Julianna continues sticking stickers on her parents' newly painted bathroom walls. Lauren, Julianna's mom, will take stickers instead of what Julianna was doing yesterday... smearing poop.

Billy, 5-year-old, boy:

"Sport! Can you turn off the TV and go practice your guitar?"

"No."

Billy continues watching "Spidey and His Amazing Friends."

Sasha, 7-year-old, girl:

"Hey Sasha. Can you go clean your room, please?"

"No."

Sasha continues playing with her Hot Wheels.

Peter, 8-year-old, boy:

"Would you like to go play with Brynnley?"

"No thanks."

Peter returns to the building with PicassoTiles.

Ava, 10-year-old, girl:

"*Hey! Do you think you can put the dishes away?*"

"*No.*"

Ava continues painting her masterpiece.

Ryan, 15-year-old, boy

"*Ry, Could you take out the trash?*"

"*No.*"

Ryan continues creating his YouTube video.

Justin, 40-year-old, man

"*Hey Justin, can you get me the report with the preliminary results?*"

Silence.

Justin ignores his boss and continues creating plans for world domination.

Did you notice a pattern? I mean, you probably figured it out once you the read the title...at least, I hope you kind of knew what was coming.

For some reason, some "parenting experts" have encouraged parents to be kind and ask their children to do something. But here is the biggest issue: if you give the child an opportunity to use their very favorite word, they will use it. No qualms! Chances are they're doing something they want to do, and you're going to ask them to do something they don't wanna.

When you ask your child to do something, instead of telling them to do it, you're opening the door for the equal opportunity response, "No."

Your child is not at the same level as you. Each family has a hierarchy*. Yes, every family. You can either be at the top leading your family, or you can have your child calling all the shots. One leads to better family functioning, and the other well...to my office, to the office of another marriage and family therapist, or in the most severe cases, to a juvenile detention center.

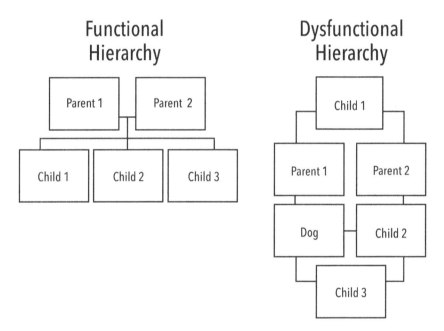

By asking someone to do something, you're implying they have a choice in the matter. And well, more times than not, they will not choose the choice you wanted them to.

My husband falls prey to this problem all the damn time. And guess what I do every time? My head hangs and I laugh because I know what their response will be—"No."

---

*A family funtivity: Draw your family hierarchy.

Now, when it comes to your spouse, you should ask him/her questions, like, "Hey, honey, can you bring me my book?" because they are on the same level as you in the family hierarchy, or at least they should be.

If the person is higher or at the same level as you, then you ask them to do things. If the person is beneath you in the hierarchy, then you tell them to do things.

See how that works?

 Get the child's attention. Pause the show. Have them stop doing what they're doing and look at you. You may need to make physical contact—think a gentle hand on their shoulder.

 Tell them specifically what you want them to do. Start the sentence with a verb and use as few words as you can.

For example:

"Clean your room."

"Take out trash."

"Complete your homework."

"Flush the toilet."

"Play with Brynnley."

"Eat your dinner."

"Put shoes on."

Apparently, you get extra parenting points if you can reduce your instruction to three words...

Okay, and now I can guess some of you may be having some feels about the abruptness and the lack of niceties. If this is you, you aren't alone (my editor is with you); feel free to add in a "please" and "thank you" to your three-word command. After all, they are the magic words.

FIVE SECOND RULE

A family of three finishes dinner at the kitchen table on a Sunday evening. During dinner Steph, the mother, excitedly told Bruce, her husband, and Melissa, their six-year-old daughter, all about her girls trip to Savannah, Georgia that she just returned from that afternoon. She was gone for four days and missed their previous therapy session.

After dinner, Melissa headed into the living room and played with dolls. Bruce entered the office to catch up on some work that he avoided to spend more time with Melissa when Steph was gone. Steph went to the kitchen and washed dishes.

"Mel, bring your plate, cup, and silverware to the kitchen, please,"

Steph commanded in an average volume and pleasant voice.

Melissa continued playing with her dolls as if she hadn't heard anything.

Steph noticed Mel has not complied with her command and not two seconds after she finished her last statement raised her voice,

"Mel! Bring plate, cup, and silverware to kitchen."

Melissa turned her head towards Steph and paused. Steph was not satisfied with her daughter's lack of compliance, and within three seconds of finishing her last command, crossed into the living room and shouted at Melissa.

"MELISSA GRACE! YOU WILL LISTEN TO ME! STOP PLAYING! GO! TAKE YOUR PLATE, CUP, AND SILVERWARE TO THE SINK! NOW!"

Melissa looked up at Steph and paused again.

Two seconds after Steph finished her last yell, she crossed the small distance between her and Melissa and grabbed the doll from Melissa's hand, threw it on the table, then grabbed Melissa's arm and pulled her to her feet. Melissa yanked her arm free and yelled back,

"I HEARD YOU! GIVE ME A SECOND!"

"OH, YOU HEARD ME? WHICH TIME?"

Bruce was sitting in the office listening to his wife and daughter get into yet another one of their tiffs.

He thought,

"Why is Steph not using the five second rule Andrea taught us this week in session?"

"WOW!

"Is that really what we sound like when we don't give Melissa 5-seconds to respond?

"OH! Steph was in Savannah and I didn't have time to teach her the 5 second rule!

"I'll wait and see how this plays out and I'll pull Steph aside in a little bit and tell her about the 5 second rule. Because, yeah, this tiff could have been avoided."

Melissa slowly moved to the kitchen table, grabbed her plate, cup, and silverware, and put them in the sink. Shot her mother a snide look and asked,

"May I return to playing with my dolls, mother dearest?"

Steph, still heated, raised her finger, pointed it at Melissa's face, and responded with,

> "You will do a better job of doing what I say when I say it, young lady!"

Melissa sighed and returned to the living room and played with her dolls.

Steph, angry washed the dishes. Then she headed to the office and asked Bruce,

> "Can you believe the nerve of your daughter?!"

Bruce stopped his work, turned in his chair, faced Steph and said,

> "Well, there's a technique we covered in session with Andrea this week that probably would have prevented that incident from escalating like it did. I forgot to teach it to you. I'm sorry."

> "What?! Are you seriously blaming your daughter not listening to me on me?"

> "I'm not blaming you or our daughter. I'm simply suggesting you let me tell you about the 5 second rule so you can see for yourself why what just happened, happened and how it can be prevented in the future."

> "FINE! I'm listening."

When you give your child any instruction, allow them five seconds to act before you repeat yourself. Their brains need time to hear what you're saying, process the information, and then get their bodies moving.

BUT if you keep giving them the same instruction over and over and over again, rapid fire style, they have to keep processing what you're saying...which just delays what you really want to have happen—them complying with your command.

Believe me, I get it. You give them an instruction and you want them to comply right here and now. But their auditory loops need time to process.

Let me give you a real-life situation to help understand what your child is experiencing.

Imagine a time when someone said something to you, you said, "What?!" Then you heard what they said in your mind, but it's too late, they've already repeated themselves. So, you have to wait until they're done, process that quicker, because you already know what they said, and then respond. That is your auditory loop. Both hemispheres of your brains need time to process what people are saying.

Here are the steps for giving a command to your child while honoring the 5 Second Rule:

   Give them the command.

   Take a breathe.

   Count to five in your head. Slowly.
NOT onetwothreefourfive,
but one...two...three...four...five.

   If the child hasn't responded after you count to five, then give them the instruction again.

   Count to five again in your head.

Then, if they still haven't started to do what you want them to do, it's time for hand over hand.

Give them the five seconds—it'll save your sanity and your relationship with your child.

Steph has mastered the five second rule, but occasionally struggles with parenting Melissa because, well Melissa inherited Steph's more oppositional nature. We joke about this frequently in session. And if you remember Taylor from the "One Size Doesn't Fit All" parenting tip, children who are "feisty, do the opposite of what they are told, or have 'BIG' personalities" require parents who are "firm in commands, freedom to explore, allow strengths to shine, and don't show when they've bested you."

Speaking of feisty kids, wait until you read the next story.

HAND OVER HAND

The clock striked 7:00pm.

Jim announced,

"Alright. It's time to clean up."

I walked upstairs and began folding the massive pile of unfolded clothes across three hampers.

Our twins, Charlotte and Connor, immediately stopped what they were doing and began cleaning up. Chloe, our youngest, 3 years old at the time, on the other hand, pretended she didn't just hear her father, who has a booming voice, say "clean up," and continued building a crib with Picasso Tiles for JJ from Cocomelon.

Jim walked to the entrance of the playroom and said,

"Chlo, it's time to clean."

"Old McDonald had a farm, ee i ee i oh! And on that farm he had a sheep, ee i ee i oh! With a BAA BAA here. And a BAA BAA there. Here a BAA BAA. There a BAA BAA. Everywhere a BAA BAA. Old McDonald had a farm, ee i ee i oh!"

Jim walked towards her so that he was in front of her, bent down, made eye contact, and commanded,

"Chloe Noelle. Can you please clean*?"

Chloe striked her signature move of crossing her arms, sticking her chin in the air, turning away from Jim, and ignored him.

---

*See what I mean from "Tell. Don't Ask." Every single time.

> "Chloe, if you start cleaning up right now, you can still earn your life saver gummie."

Chloe maintained her signature pose. Jim grabbed JJ, the Picasso Tiles crib, and some other near-by toys, gathered them into a pile, pointed to it, and said,

> "Here is your pile. When you clean this pile up, then you're done."

Chloe, demonstrating why we gave her the family nickname of "Troublemaker," continued to ignore Jim.

Jim realized she isn't cleaning on her own and prepares himself for hand over hand. He closed his eyes, took a few deep breaths while simultaneously bringing his shoulders down away from his ears, and paused. He walked over and grabbed a toy bin and kneeled back down in front of her. Once he felt cool, calm and collected, he commanded,

> "Chloe, it's time for hand over hand."

He extended his left hand and gently placed it over the top of her right hand. Then he guided her right hand down to JJ's peas and gently encouraged her to close her small, yet sweaty, hand around the toy. The two of them moved the peas and hovered it over the toy bin, and then Jim loosened his grip, encouraging Chloe to drop the toy into the bin with a "clunk."

Jim made eye contact, smiled, and praised Chloe with

> "Thank you, Chloe for cleaning up. Let's do one more toy together and then you can clean the rest of your pile."

The hand over hand process was repeated, this time over JJ. Jim praised Chloe again for cleaning up, and released her hand.

> "Here is the rest of your toy pile that I expect you to clean up.

When the pile of toys is gone, then you are done cleaning."

Jim waited to see her next move.

She hesitated, starred at Jim, no doubt – weighing her options. She extended her arm, grabbed a Picasso Tile, and plopped it into the toy bin.

"Good job cleaning up your Picasso Tile, Chlo."

Chloe's manner shifted and she began cleaning up.

Jim lifted off his knees, convinced that she will clean the rest of her pile, and waited for her to finish.

"Thank you, Chloe Bo Boloe for cleaning your pile. You did not earn a life saver gummie because you did not start cleaning when I asked you to. But how about a high five?"

Chloe smiled at her father's term of endearment, became a little sad that she didn't earn a treat, but settled for the high five. She looked to see where her father's open hand was, propelled her open hand, and made contact.

"Now, let's go get vitamins."

"Piggyback ride, daddy?"

Jim nodded, kneeled, waited for Chloe to hop on, and then away they went.

Almost all children, if not all children, will demonstrate oppositional and defiant behavior. But this is unacceptable behavior. I've NEVER met a parent who was like, "Yeah, I don't mind when my child doesn't do what I tell them to do." Oppositional and defiant behavior is not allowed.

Why?

Because getting our child to comply with our commands is essentially the foundation of intentional parenting. If you can't get them to do what they are told, well, shit! You got nothing! No stable foundation. You might as well be standing in quicksand.

Therefore, our child doesn't get to decide to not carry their weight and simply sass us out of cleaning up, or any other command we give them. NOPE! Ain't happening on my watch! So, what's a parent to do with oppositional and defiant behavior?

Hand over hand.

The key to this technique is remaining cool as a cucumber. If you feel any fire in your belly (sorry, remember, I'm a clinical CHILD psychologist), then you do not attempt this move until you have pulled yourself together.

I repeat!

Do not attempt hand over hand until you're as cool as a cucumber.

Once you're cool as a cucumber, take your child's hand in yours and gently direct them (not tugging yet, at least) to complete the task you have commanded them to complete. Once they perform an aspect of the task, even with your assistance, you praise them. If they show signs of willingness to comply, then gradually remove your assistance, and continue praising the desired behavior.

Keep in mind, depending on how much opposition and defiance your child possesses, they may not show signs of willingness to comply. In that case, continue completing the task with your hand on top of theirs, and praise once the two of you complete the task.

If you are sitting there on your porcelain throne thinking, "Andrea, what if they run away, physically resist, or become aggressive when I place my hand on their hand?"

Here is what I want you to try:

 Remain cool as a cucumber.

 Tell them, "That is not an option. Your options right now are to complete the task by yourself or with my help."

 Use as little force as necessary to get them to return to the task and complete it.

 Ignore any desire to get into a verbal argument with your child. Stick to the phrase in the second poop point.

 Praise any sign of willingness to comply.

Know this may take you returning your child to the task multiple times. It can be exhausting and frustrating. If at any time, you feel fire in your belly (or wherever you experience anger and frustration), then do something that is going to bring you back to your cool as a cucumber state. But please do not let the child escape doing what you commanded them to do. No one wins that way.

Remember, parenting is a front-loaded activity, a little bit (or a lot) of work now, goes a LONG way later.

Chloe is and will always be our feisty child. Jim and I've accepted that and we love her feistiness (when she isn't being feisty when we tell her to do something). My sister-in-law once sent me an Instagram post that stated, "My daughter will change the world, as long as I survive raising her." And this is 100% Chloe.

She started preschool this year and has the same teacher as Charlotte and Connor had. On the "Tell me about your child" sheet, I wrote, "If you're expecting Charlotte and Connor, DON'T!"

Within the first two weeks of preschool starting, two different people commented to Jim how different Chloe is compared to the twins.

YEP!

BONUS! Practical ways to get kids to clean rooms:

 Create piles. Create smaller piles of the toys. Just kind of move them into smaller "bite size" piles. Then have the child clean up one pile at a time. Maybe taking a dance break between piles. Or running a lap. Or reading a book.

 Give the child a time limit. This increases the urgency a child will feel and prevent the lollygagging that our children LOVE exhibiting. Once the time has passed, if the room is adequately cleaned, then give them a reward (See Positive Reinforcement, Your First Line of Defense for ideas).

YOUR CHILD, THE ESCAPE ARTIST

Katniss, an eight-year-old precocious girl, played happily in her room. You can't see the floor because all her toys, or what appeared to be all her quivers, bows, and arrows were strewn everywhere.

Dr. Everdeen, Katniss's mother, walked upstairs and tried to open Katniss's door. I say "tried" because she had to put some force behind opening the door from all the toys blocking it.

Once Dr. Everdeen finally got the door open, she stepped over and around toys, with her hands raised in exasperation, and said,

> "Katniss, this place is a disaster! Please clean it."

Dr. Everdeen turned, maneuvered her way back through the toys, closed the door, and returned to working on her lecture for the next day. After about 30 minutes, a reasonable amount of time for an eight-year-old to clean her room, Dr. Everdeen stopped working on her lecture, walked back up the stairs, forced the door open, and found the room in the same state it was 30 minutes ago.

Now a little agitated, Dr. Everdeen, with a much sterner voice said,

> "Katniss, did you hear me before? I told you to clean your room. You've done absolutely nothing besides play and make more of a mess. I can't believe you haven't cleaned up a SINGLE toy!"

Katniss looked up at her agitated mother and froze. She then dropped her head, slumped her shoulders and whispered,

"I'm dumb."

Hearing her daughter engage in negative self-talk, Dr. Everdeen closed the gap between her and her daughter, dropped to her knees, cupped Katniss's chin, raised it and said,

"Oh sweetie. You're not dumb."

Mom guilt boiled up inside Dr. Everdeen. How could she selfishly be prepping a lecture, not engaging with her child, and now her only child believes she is dumb. What kind of mom does that?

Dr. Everdeen lovingly grabbed her daughter's hand and brought her out of the toy-strewn room (managing to only step on one Lego but muffled the pain sound) and downstairs. She led Katniss to the couch, pulled Katniss onto her lap, made eye contact, and then asked,

"Honey, why do you think you're dumb?"

Katniss was quiet for a little while, shrugged her shoulders, and then meekly said,

"I don't know."

Dr. Everdeen hugged Katniss, told her,

"Well, I don't think you're dumb. You're a brilliant young girl. You know that, right?"

Katniss smiled the littlest of smiles and tucked in for another hug.

Dr. Everdeen stroked Katniss's hair and asked,

"Do you want to draw on the coffee table next to me as I finish up my lecture for tomorrow?

Then I can make us your favorite lunch—pizza bagels."

Katniss perked right up and got super excited because drawing is her absolute favorite thing to do in the whole world.

And just like that mother and daughter went about their day together—toy-strewn room still messy as ever...

There you have it.

Have you figured out the why of Katniss's behavior?

If you guessed escape/avoidance, you would be right.

As your reward, one of your children's names have been removed from the reaping bowl. Which child will you save?

The why of Katniss's behavior is escape/avoidance because she used negative self-talk to distract her mother and escape the task of cleaning her room.

Katniss was playing happily in her room. Who wants that to end to just clean up all the toys?

Not me. And not Katniss.

So, she said she's dumb. That stopped her highly educated mother in her tracks, distracted her from being upset at Katniss for not listening or cleaning up, activated her mom guilt, and put her mom into a stance of nurturing. Katniss got out of cleaning up and got to move on to something she loves doing—drawing, and devouring pizza bagels.

If your child can get out of something, they will, by any means necessary. It is our job as the parent to not let them get out of expectations, chores, tasks, etc. just because they don't want to do it. If we continuously allow them out of things they have to do for things they want to do, that's when we fast forward 15 years and they lack self-discipline or the ability to delay gratification: in other words, they become adult babies who live in your basement. And our society can't handle any more adult babies.

Now, I remember during the second session, when Katniss's mother was going over the data she collected on Katniss's self-talk. Her jaw about hit the floor when she realized all the instances over the last week that Katniss was able to get out of being lectured at (both Katniss's parents are professors), earning a consequence, or a chore because she used negative self-talk.

Here are some other statements Katniss used:

"You don't love me."

"I'm the one in the family that everyone hates."

Can you pinpoint any escape-artist phrases your child may be using on you? Write them here:

_____

_____

_____

_____

_____

The most common escape-artist phrases tend to hit us at our core because our child has learned over time that saying these things puts us into an off-kilter state and they can use that to their advantage.

Which raised a very valid question that Dr. Everdeen posed during that second conversation. She looked at me and, in complete despair, asked,

"Does Katniss know that she is doing this?"

My guess is the actual question behind this question was, "Is Katniss a sociopath?"

And the answer to the actual question is...no. Our children are not sociopaths or psychopaths, but remember, they are savages. They have simply learned through experiences that they can say things or do things (cry, yell, throw a temper tantrum, etc.) that put them on offense and you on defense.

What we need to do is become aware of their escape-artist phrases and behaviors and not let them escape their responsibilities.

Here are some phrases to respond with when you notice they used an escape-artist phrase:

- "I understand you are _____ (insert a guess at their feeling), but the expectation right now is for you to _____. Once you are done with that, then we can talk more about your thoughts and your feelings."

- WHEN you finish _____, THEN you can do _____.

- "You do what you need to do before you do what you want to do."

Dr. Everdeen now knew Katniss's escape-artist phrases, stopped them dead in their tracks, and we successfully ended therapy a few sessions later.

THE 4 R'S OF LOGICAL CONSEQUENCES

Colton, a 12-year-old boy, and his adoptive father, Chris, and Taya, Chris's wife, entered my therapy room.

Yeah, let's pause and cover that again. Colton's biological parents were no longer in his life. He was now being raised by his adoptive father, who was originally his stepfather, Chris, and his stepfather turned adoptive father's new wife, Taya.

And if that wasn't interesting enough, Colton was closest to Taya and relatively estranged from Chris.

"What brings you all in today?"

Chris immediately responded with,

"Well, ma'am, the boy is having a hard time at school and doesn't mind himself in my home."

"What does him not minding himself in your home look like, Chris?"

"He doesn't make his bed. Leaves his dirty dishes on the table. Doesn't take out the trash when he is told. Drops his bag in the middle of the entryway. Rolls his eyes. And talks back. All these behaviors are unacceptable, ma'am."

"When Colton does these things, how do you and Taya respond?"

"I make him write or do push-ups, ma'am."

I saw Taya make uncomfortable movements, guessed she didn't agree with Chris's disciplinary strategies, paused, collected myself, and questioned,

"I see. What do you have Colton write?"

Chris puffed his chest out and proudly announced,

"If he rolls his eyes at me, I make him write, 'I will not roll my eyes' 100 times, ma'am."

"100 times?"

"Yes, ma'am."

"Uh. Okay. And tell me more about the push-ups."

"If he talks back or yells at Taya or me, then I make him do 100 push-ups, ma'am."

I tried to cut the tension by smiling slyly, and sarcastically asked,

"You like the number 100, dontcha?"

Everyone laughed and Colton added,

"You have no idea."

"Don't forget 'ma'am,' boy."

"Well, Colton. I bet your penmanship is the best in your grade, and I can see you have arm muscles for days."

Again, everyone laughed.

Chris sat up a little taller, perceiving that to be a compliment... little did he know.

Does this type of discipline sound like something?

If you guessed the discipline we typically associate with the military, you would be correct. Chris was a retired Marine and all his years in service strongly influenced his parenting practices.

Please know, I am not talking ill of our military. I greatly appreciate our military and the men and women who serve and protect our country...I love all of my freedoms afforded to me as a tax paying American.

But let's get something straight: the mission of our military is to train soldiers. Their disciplinary practices reflect this mission. Our mission as parents is not to raise soldiers, OR at least my mission is not to raise soldiers.

If this is your mission as a parent, maybe you should stop reading this book because you're going to be greatly disappointed.

If your mission as a parent is to raise well-adjusted children who become well-adjusted teens who then become well-adjusted adults who contribute positively to society, well, then keep reading (I mean you only have one more third to go...you might as well).

Anyway, as you can probably already tell, this disciplinary practice, that was molded by Chris being ex-military, was not working for this family. Or else they wouldn't have been in a therapy room. And don't get me wrong, there were other issues going on for Colton and his family, but the first issue I set out to address was replacing the use of illogical consequences with logical consequences.

Logical consequences are those where the disciplinary action directly addresses the behavior that grinds our gears.

When implementing a consequence, remember the 4 R's of logical consequences:

RELATED: The consequence is related to the infraction. The assigned consequence will help the child either improve on that specific behavior or it will cause the child to think of whether they want that consequence in the future.

For example, I get really frustrated with youth sports coaches when they punish their athletes by having them run for everything. When I was a high school basketball player, for every free throw we missed in a game, we were required to run a 9 (the width of the court 9 times in under 36 seconds). How is running a 9 helping us hit our free throws? It doesn't.

A logical consequence would have been requiring us to make 25 free throws for every free throw missed in the game.

RESPECTFUL: One of our main goals with discipline should always be doling out a consequence while not dinging the relationship. We do not shame our child.

For example, I see on social media parents who force their two children who have fought to wear an oversized t-shirt. The children always seem incredibly unhappy—dinging the relationship. And finally, the parent's post has an air of smugness to it—reminiscent of posts seen on dogshaming.com*.

REASONABLE: It should be enough to teach them the lesson you

---

*For those of you not familiar with this website, people would post a picture of their dog after they did something "bad". The picture would include a sign that explained what the dog did.

One of my favs: a small, curly white haired dog, named Chloe with a sign that read, "I ate one my Mommy's diamond earrings yesterday and now she must dig through my poop to find it. Do I feel bad? Not one bit. Would I do it again? More than likely if given the change to."

Maybe it's something about the name, Chloe...

want them to learn, but not overboard. You want it to "hurt" or be "painful" but not ridiculous.

For example, when parents ground their children for months on end. Is that really necessary? To me, I find grounding anything over a week or two to be excessive. I always like to encourage parents to set a time frame and then allow their child to knock days off the grounding by engaging in prosocial behaviors related to the infraction. Reinforcement, baby! It's the best way to modify behavior.

REVEALED IN ADVANCE: Tell the child ahead of time what the consequence will be if they exhibit certain behaviors. This cuts down on tantrums and allows your child to decide whether or not the act is "worth" the price.

For example, parents get confused when their child freaks out when they implement a consequence out of left field. You know if you are caught speeding that you will get a ticket. Do you throw a tantrum when a police officer gives you a ticket for going 85 mph in a 65 mph zone? NO! Because you broke the law, now you gotta pay your fine. I encourage parents to have conversations with their children about behavioral expectations, and, within that conversation, state what is the consequence for violating that specific behavioral expectation. Something like this: "If you post unapproved content on your social media, you will lose all social media privileges for 7 days.

Some of my favorite logical consequences:

 Expecting children to clean up messes after they spill

 Requiring children to change their own sheets and clothes when they wet the bed or pee/poop in their pants

Losing phone privileges for a period of time (think in days, not weeks or months) when they violate an expectation about their phone

 Cleaning up their room if they made it look like a tornado tore through it

All of my favorite logical consequences follow the 4 R's of logical consequences. They are:

 Related

 Respectful

 Reasonable

 Revealed in Advance

Logical consequences may be the trickiest parenting practice to become second nature. We're fighting against our natural inclination to fight, flight, or freeze. I highly recommend giving yourself some slack. They become easier with practice, I promise. It's the whole parenting is a front-loaded activity. Put in the time and energy to think through the 4 R's of logical consequences now to reap the benefits later when your child is a teen and comes home late.

You may be wondering, "What happened with Colton, Chris and Taya? Were you able to break Chris of illogical consequences and save Colton from needing shoulder surgery from all the push-ups?"

I'd love to say, "DAMN SKIPPY!" But I can't. The family saw me for a few sessions.

I tried to reason with Chris about using logical consequences, but, when push came to shove, his military training was too strong.

You win some, you lose some.

TIRED OF NAGGING? USE NATURAL CONSEQUENCES

Let's go back to 1BC, not before Christ, but before COVID. It was a Sunday in March in Northwest Ohio, where it's blistering cold and windy, and my family was getting ready for church. We were at the point most parents dread, at least if you are similar to us and have twin 2.5-year-olds and a 6-month-old—we wanted the kids to put their shoes and coats on. Charlotte, our girl twin, put her shoes and coat on with no grief. As did Chloe, the baby, but...does she really have a choice? Connor, our boy twin, was another story.

He looked at us and said, *"No."*

I bent down, made eye contact, and said,

> *"Bud, it's really cold outside. And we have to walk a really long distance (imagine the length of a football field) to get into church. And you're going to be cold."*

He looked at me, and responded with, *"No."*

Jim, the mechanical engineer, looked at me and said,

> *"You're the clinical child psychologist. What do we do?"*

I paused, glared at Jim and said,

> *"Natural consequences."*

We got the twins, the baby, and ourselves into the car, Connor sans any outerwear. And as we walked towards church that day, in that cold weather, about 15 yards in, Connor whined,

> *"Mama, I'm cold."*

I bent down, made eye contact, wrapped my arm around his waist, and said,

> "Bud, I told you to get your coat on, but you chose not to listen. If you promise, to put your coat on when I tell you to, I'll let you come under my poncho with me."

He looked at me with a little chatter in his teeth, and replied,

> "I promise, Mama."

I picked him up, put him under my poncho and we walked the rest of the distance cuddled together.

Natural consequences are a way to parent without nagging.

Who likes to be nagged?

Nobody.

And who enjoys nagging?

Surely, I don't.

Natural consequences allow people to learn from the consequences that naturally come from the choices they make. And as parents, natural consequences allow us to maintain a high-quality relationship with our kids because we aren't nagging them.

We allow them to learn from their mistakes. We allow them to fail[*].

But therein lies the challenge because as parents, we don't want them to struggle. I get it. We want them to succeed.

---

[*]If you are looking for a great book specifically on allowing your child to fail, I highly recommend *The Gift of Failure* by Jessica Lahey.

But you're doing them a disservice if you don't incorporate natural consequences into your parenting because it allows them to learn without you ever having to say a word. They learn and you don't ding the relationship. It's a win-win.

But here is my caveat. You only use natural consequences if the consequence is not serious injury or death.

I'm not advocating you hanging back and allowing your 4-year-old to cross the street without looking and they get hit by a car.

Common sense here, people!

There is no guideline to determine this. It's all about what you're comfortable with. Some parents are comfortable with their child breaking their arm because they were climbing a tree, got cocky or distracted, and mis-stepped. Other parents don't even want their child to scrap their knees. You must figure out where your comfort level is.

But death should be off e'rybody's table.

I'm just saying.

One of the coolest things about natural consequences is they don't solely work for the parent-child relationship. They work on significant others, siblings, employees, and dogs. Because, again, no one likes to be nagged.

Some of my favorite natural consequences include:

 Children getting their fingers pinched in drawers

 Children being cold because they refused to put their coats or other outerwear on

 Children earning bad grades because they chose

not to do their homework or study for their tests

 Children being teased by their peers for being the smelly kid

 Children being late because they struggle to manage their time (you give them a specific time, if they ain't there, you leave without them, granted they are old enough to be left alone)

The next time you see your child about to do something that's not a wise choice or fail, here are the steps for using natural consequences:

 Catch yourself

 Close your mouth

 Watch it happen

 If and when it's appropriate, ask them, "What did you learn?"

This ain't easy, but sometimes you have to let nature take its course.

Now let's fast forward to April 2020. Again, we were getting ready to leave the house, but this time it's just me. Jim was at work. So now I have twin 3.5-year-olds and a 1.5 year old. I instructed the kids to get their shoes and coats on.

Charlotte and Chloe went to the closet, grabbed their shoes and coats, and put them on.

I glared at Connor, waited 5-seconds, and repeated,

"Connor, Bud, get your coat on."

He paused, because at the end of the day he's still a rascal, gave me a sly look, and said,

"Okay, Mama."

He grabbed his shoes and coat and put them on. And out the door we went to have a great day.

What do you say?

Hey! Hey!

THE WARM AND FUZZIES

YOUR RATIO'S OFF

"Daddy's the WORST!"

This statement or some iteration of it plagued our household for numerous weeks. The statement solely came from our 5-year-old son, Connor. It was on Easter Sunday that, Jim, and I decided to explore these statements with Connor.

Jim started by asking,

"Connor, son, what makes Daddy the worst?"

"You're not fair."

"Tell me a time I wasn't fair."

"Hmmm."

I interjected with,

"Connor, Bud, are you saying Daddy isn't fair because he took away your episode in the morning?"

"YES!"

"But, Bud, you know that Daddy is not taking away your episode. You're behaving in a way that gets your episode in the morning taken away. So, let's create a plan for how you can go back to earning your episode in the morning on a consistent basis. How does that sound?"

Jim quickly interjects with,

"Wait! I'm confused. Mama takes away your episode and you may say that she's the worst Mama ever, but you only say it that night and it never comes up again during the day. Why is that?"

What was going on? Why could I do the same thing Jim did with the same exact kid, but not be consistently labeled as the worst mama ever?! It took me writing this parenting tip to realize what was going on*.

Jim didn't have enough positive interactions with Connor banked. Yes, Connor occasionally will tell me that I am the worst mama, but it is rare, and it goes away as soon as he is no longer in emotional mind.

I'm the fun parent. I'm the parent that takes the kids places. Each month, I take one of them on a date. I'm the engaged parent. It's different with Jim. Jim is more disengaged. He works longer hours and the hours that he has with the kids alone consists of picking them up from my parents, cooking them dinner, dinner, and then bedtime. Where's the fun?

Don't get me wrong, I'm not a perfect parent. I make mistakes. There are times when I yell at my children, but I have banked a lot of positive interactions with them to counter the negative interactions with them. This is called the positive to negative interaction ratio.

When I do make a parenting mistake, I literally use a coping thought and tell myself, "MAN! It's okay, I have so many positives banked."

What is this magic ratio I speak of?

John Gottman, a marriage expert, has discovered that the number one factor of whether a marriage will survive is if the couple maintains a 5 to 1 positive to negative interactions ratio.

---

*There's a reason why mental health therapists don't practice on their family and friends—they're not objective.

What does this mean? For every one negative interaction you have with your partner, you must have five positive interactions to make up for that one negative interaction. I simply extend the ratio to parenting.

We want to maintain a 5 to 1 positive to negative interactions with our children.

Parenting can and should be fun. It should not solely be transactional. Research shows that fathers are more likely to be the fun parent and mothers tend to be the nurturing one who ensures the child's survival—I get it.

We grew them in our bodies. Our bodies got DESTROYED by pregnancy and labor, we don't want to waste all that hard work. But it is okay for mothers to have fun, too.

I love being the fun parent. I remember there was this one time when I took all three of my children to the local gymnastics center for toddler free time. At the end of the hour, I would gather my three children, hold their hands, and then we would run a final lap around the floor.

After a few weeks, other children would join us—imagine a huge human chain of me and ten kids. And one day, one of the other moms who spent the time socializing with other moms or on her phone—not engaging with their children, looked at me and said, "Thanks for bringing the fun!"

I simply turned, looked at her, and said, "You're welcome."

What I really wanted to say was, "You know you could bring the fun, too!"

 Put your damn cell phone down

 Get outside of your comfort zone

Channel your inner child

 Engage with your child

Now, what if your ratio is skewed, but in a different way? Where your positive interactions FAR outweigh your negative interactions.

Keep reading.

We don't want that either.

Why?

Because then we run the risk of being too lenient or having too high of expectations to never make mistakes and be the perfectly positive parent. These two extremes are not what becoming an intentional parent is about, either.

Let's tease each of these misguided ratio paths apart.

First, being too lenient. I do not want you focusing on your ratio to the detriment that you forget all the parenting tips from the high expectations section in this book and you start letting everything slide.

Your child kicks the babysitter.

Your child yells at you all the time.

Your child smears poop all over your freshly painted walls.

This is not what we want. I don't want you to become the laisse-faire, everything is peachy-keen, Pollyanna parent. Being the laisse-faire parent who sets no boundaries, does not set their child up for success. You become the doormat. I don't want you to be your child's doormat. I want your children to respect you because you set clear high expectations and enforce those expectations, but also bring the fun and then the warm and fuzzies.

Second, I don't want you to be the parent who feels like they must be the perfectly positive parent and beats yourself up because you made a parenting mistake. If this is you, please re-read "All Is Not Lost." Having these unrealistically high expectations increases the chances that we will experience anxiety—making you becoming an intentional parent significantly more challenging because the anxiety is eating up your cognitive bandwidth.

So, the next time you and one of your children's relationships is struggling:

 Ask yourself, "What's my ratio with this child?"

 If your answer is more negatives than is ideal: keep reading. There may be something that will help. If none of that helps, then bring the fun, plan some quality time, or go on a date.

 If your answer is too many positives than is ideal: use the coping thought, "My child should not like me 100% of the time" and reread any of the parenting tips from the high expectations section of this book that seem to fit.

Since the drafting of this parenting tip, Jim has become more fun! He plays games with the kids between dinner and bedtime a few times each week. And they LOVE to roughhouse with him–stay tuned for this practical tip later on.

BONUS:

Ways to bring the fun without adding extra time:

Make ordinary things (walks to school, driving, mealtimes, bedtime) fun by dancing, singing, and playing games.

Help the Not Fun Parent Out:

Buy them "*Questions for Humans—Kids Edition*"

Tap into their interests and expertise. People tend to be able to be more fun when it's within areas they know a lot about. I can't make mechanical engineering fun (I don't know what my husband does half the time), but Jim sure can by building intricate designs with legos and making the best and most aerodynamic paper airplanes!

Parent and child dates. On a regular basis (whatever works for you and your family), the not fun parent takes the child out on a date. Let the child take the lead and choose what you do. I've done this the last two years and it's amazing what I learn about each of my kids during our dates.

BE WHERE YOU SAY YOU'RE GOING TO BE

"She thinks my tractor's sexy. It really turns her on."

Andre, one of my favorite clients ever, serenaded me.

"You know you're a 12-year-old Black boy, right?"

I teased and gave him a playful look.

Andre shot me a sly smile, threw a soft ball at me, and continued, this time louder with,

"She's always starin' at me. While I'm chugging along."

I allowed it because I knew the truth.

The truth being that him singing was his defense mechanism, protecting him from the hurt he was experiencing.

Andre paused, looked down at the floor, and asked quietly,

"Dr. Dre, you think he's coming?"

"I don't know, Andre."

I can't even say, "I hope so" anymore because Andre and I have been burned by his father too many times, five times to be exact, and I can't stand to see him hurt more.

"How 'bout we give him 5 more minutes and then I'll call?"

"Thanks, Dr. Dre."

Andre's head was still down, but ten seconds later, he looked up, with his big toothy smile and asked,

"Can I show you a new video?"

Andre and I shared a love of music videos, and he was always willing to share a new one.

"Bet!"

Andre jumped into the computer chair and brought my dinosaur of a computer to life and pulled up the video.

The five minutes ticked down. As the video ended, I picked up the receiver, dialed the number, took a deep breath, and prayed that Andre's dad answered.

"Hello?"

"Hey, Earl. It's Dr. Andrea Mata. Andre and I are in my office wondering how far away you are?"

I felt Andre's eyes burning into the back of my head. I tried not to make eye contact, because, as good as my ability to maintain a stoic face was, I didn't trust it not to give away the incredible amount of anger and frustration I experienced towards Earl and his lack of one of my core values, "Give a shit."

"Oh! Hey, Dr. Andrea. Um...Yeah. Traffic is nuts. I'll be there in 10 minutes."

"Yeah, traffic* at this time of day is unpredictable. Drive safely. We'll see you when you get here."

I hung up and turned toward Andre, whose face could be best described as a pug who loves their owner dearly and the owner has been gone for a few hours and doesn't know when that owner will return, so he waits by the door in anticipation of hearing the car pull up—head slightly tilted, nothing but

---

*I laugh in my head when people who live in the area I was practicing from use the word "traffic." He has no idea what traffic is! Because traffic to me is it takes you an hour and a half to travel 20 miles

anticipation in their eyes, hanging on my every word.

"Well, Dr. Dre?! What did he say?"

"He'll be here in 10 minutes. Now, let's talk about that video."

I attempted distracting Andre from the uncomfortableness of whether his dad would stand us up for a sixth time and showed Andre that there are adults out there that show up and care about him because at that moment, and at that point in his life, that was exactly what he needed.

Fifteen minutes passed and Earl wasn't there yet.

Andre grew more and more defeated.

A few more minutes passed, I accepted that Earl wasn't showing up, that he lied to us again, and thought, "I preferred when he would ghost us and not show up at all or not answer my phone calls. But the fact that he answered the phone and said he would be there in ten minutes, having no intention of showing up, was downright awful."

I was enraged, but, being the therapist, I knew if I was enraged, I could only imagine what Andre was feeling, and it wasn't about me. It was about him. So, I did the only thing I could think of. I reached under my desk, grabbed my basketball, turned towards Andre, and asked,

"Hoop?"

"Yeah" was the only response Andre could muster.

After reading this, I think the tip is pretty self-explanatory—

 Show up when you say you're going to.

 Don't make promises you can't keep.

 If you say you're going to do something or if you're going to be somewhere—do it or be there!

This is how trust is built—by the little things. All relationships need trust. It's a cornerstone. If you don't have that, well, then you got nothing.

Parent with integrity. Don't promise anything unless you know with 100% confidence that you can do it. Before you make a promise, stop, pause, and ask yourself, "Can I comply with what I'm about to promise my child?"

If you can't say yes, then don't promise it. It's okay to tell them you're going to try to do something or try to be somewhere. Adjust your language.

If you continually don't do what you say you're going to do or be where you say you are going to be, then your child can't trust you. And then, boy, you found yourself in a similar situation as Liam and Mitch. This will lead to relationship problems down the line for your child.

And let's be real, there'll be times when you say you'll do something, but don't. Or you say you'll be somewhere, but you're not. We are humans after all. None of us are parenting gods, me included. I make mistakes.

But own those times. Don't make excuses. Don't pass the responsibility off onto someone else. Own it. Apologize, and not one of those fake sorry not sorry shit kind of apologies—

"I'm sorry if you were upset/frustrated/angry." A truly heartfelt one. Where your behavior changes.

Be honest with them and yourself. I think of it as my rule of thumb with to do lists. You will most likely accomplish 70% (Yep, you guessed it, I made this stat up!) of your daily to-do list, not 100%, so instead of setting yourself up for failure, moderate how much you say you're going to accomplish and only include 70% of the things you think you can commit to.

Be like a pizza delivery driver, under promise, and over deliver. They tell you it's going to be 30 minutes, but they deliver in 20 minutes, and you're convinced they're DA best pizza delivery driver EVER!

Under promise and over deliver as a parent.

The seventh appointment with Andre and Earl was scheduled. When that Monday came, I sat in my office immediately before that session and prepared myself for Earl not showing up and what I could do to process Andre's emotions. Maybe we'd walk instead of hoopin'. Seven pm came and my office phone rang,

"Andrea, your 7:00pm is here."

I walked downstairs, retrieved Andre, and we immediately started talking about music videos. Three minutes passed and my office phone rang again,

"Andrea, the father of your 7:00pm is here."

My eyes shot open!

Andre quizzically looked at me.

"HE SHOWED UP!"

"WHAT?!"

"Your dad! He's downstairs. Now, be cool. Be cool. I'll go get him."

Apparently, the 7th time was the charm when it came to Earl. He showed up, engaged in family therapy, AND didn't threaten to punch Andre in the face* if he didn't listen.

Andre and Earl engaged in family therapy for numerous sessions and, eventually, the court placed Andre in Earl's custody permanently.

---

*Andre was in foster care because his mom punched him in the face. And when I tried therapy with her and Andre, she threatened to punch him again if he didn't listen.

GET DOWN ON THEIR LEVEL

It was a Friday night in an airport, and we were scheduled to board 20 minutes ago, but we hadn't even started yet. I sat near the gate and read a book about practicing self-compassion. A little girl, probably about seven years old—who ironically wore a shirt that said something to the effect of being grateful and thankful—repeatedly whined:

"Mommy, I don't want to wear shoes on the plane."

"Daddy, I don't want to stand here anymore."

"Argh!"

"Why aren't we getting on the plane?"

"What's taking so long?"

"Mommy!"

"Hello!"

"Daddy!"

"I want to get on the plane!"

"I want to go home."

Each time she said something, one of her parents responded dismissively. My favorite response was, *"That's a great question!"* All the while, they stood more than a foot away from her (remember we're in a crowded airport), completely upright so the little girl's face stared at their stomachs. Neither of them ever looked at her. Instead, they looked around the airport or at their phones.

I get it, the parents didn't want her to whine, and maybe they were practicing catch and ignore (Doubtful! BAA HAA HA!). But standing upright, not looking at her, and responding dismissively wasn't going to obtain the goal of getting their daughter not to whine.

So, what could they have done instead?

Got down on her level.

They could've bent down and made eye contact. And, if the girl was comfortable with touching, then they could've held her hand or wrapped their arm gently around her waist. Then calmly said, "Hey, Belle, what do you need right now?" And then listened, actually listened to what she had to say. (See "Hear What They Are Saying")

This small change of physical presence makes kids feel less intimidated. Why less intimidated?

Think about the implied power differential.

For a visual, think of yourself as David and you are trying to talk to Goliath. Is Goliath hearing anything David has to say?

Nope.

Because there's too much space between David's mouth and Goliath's ears.

How intimidating would that be?

Now, that's how your child feels—small and unimportant—when you don't bend down and get on their level. You're a giant to them, even if you're only 4'11".

After you chat, and they feel heard and validated, maybe you give them instructions you want them to do. But you aren't done quite yet. Finish up with a hug, peck on the cheek, high five, fist bump, shimmy, or whatever you and yours do to feel connected.

Now we talked about the physical difference, but I bet there is something that gets in the way of you getting down on their level—intrusive thoughts. The damn intrusive thoughts might creep in and tell you, "You don't have time to get on their level" or "You don't want to bend down—it's such a far way down." But let's spend some time reframing those intrusive thoughts.

Reframing: Time Investment. Lots of people tell themselves they don't have time to stop what they're doing and bend down and connect with their child. It's a matter of when you want to invest your time, now or later— it's not a matter of if.

You can invest the time when your kids are young to emotionally connect with them and you're preventing future problems because children who are connected to their parents, can emotionally connect with others.

Or you can use the excuse that right now you "don't have time*." But then you have to invest more time later: driving your child or teen to therapy where they'll address their lack of a foundation for emotional connection, all because you refused to connect with them. And these issues are not an easy or cheap fix, but super impactful because it has the potential to impact all their relationships, for the rest of their lives.

No biggie, right?

Those 10-30 seconds now compared to the multiple hours in

---

*Which is bullshit by the way—you have 10-30 seconds to stop what you're doing and give your child all your attention.

therapy later looks good, right?

The choice is yours.

Alright, now the other pesky intrusive thought of, "Andrea, really, I must bend all the way down and get on their 3-foot-tall level? Do you know how far that is?"

Reframing: Effort. You're getting your squats in. Your child is helping you maintain your ability to get down on the floor and back up.

Your child and I are simply following Dr. Kelly Starrett's advice* and are looking out for your functional movement ability for the long haul. We want you to maintain your physical health so that you can be active with them and your grandchildren for life.

You're welcome.

I obviously don't know what happened to this young girl after we loaded the airplane.

My guess?

She has since become a tween who her dismissive parents gave her a phone and now she spends all of her time on it. She dismisses her parent's requests for her to take out the trash, clean her room, or eat dinner with them.

Karma's a B _ T C H, ain't it?

---

*Mobility Guru. Author of *Built to Move*. Great read!

HEAR WHAT THEY ARE SAYING

Jacklyn, a blonde hair, blue-eyed 10-year-old White girl, with some of the greasiest hair I've ever seen (think Snape from the *Harry Potter* movies), waited with her grandmother, Fran, in the BoysTown* waiting room. Both sported a McKayla Maroney not-impressed face.

"Jacklyn and Fran, you two can come on back to room six."

They stood, engaged in a power struggle of who would be first. Jacklyn won because she possessed a long history of railroading Fran with her oppositional and defiant behavior—hence her stint at BoysTown. Fran shot me an exasperated look, and I responded with a validating and reassuring expression.

Jacklyn turned into room six as did Fran and me. Jacklyn slammed her little, 10-year-old body into the far seat, and immediately crossed her arms, slouched, and sighed. Fran quietly and politely sat down in the chair next to Jacklyn. And as for me, I closed the door, crossed the room and sat in the chair on the other side of the desk.

I started the family session with my typical phrase,

"So, how has the last week been?"

---

*Residential treatment facility where antisocial and aggressive youth live with a married couple and other youth to address their behaviors. It's common for the youth and their families to do family therapy to help the youth change their behaviors, and the ultimate goal is for the youth to be able to return to living with their family.

Silence. Both stared at me. I gave them a few moments—gauging who would crack first.

It was Fran with, *"Andrea! Look at her hair!!*
Y'all at BoysTown can't even get her in the shower..."

Jacklyn shot straight up in her chair and interrupted her grandmother.

"I DO SHOWER!"

"No, you don't! If you showered, your hair wouldn't be so DAMN greasy!"

"YES, I DO!"

Jacklyn became increasingly angry.

Fran looked off to the side and mumbled,

"What am I going to do? I can't believe this.
BoysTown was my last hope."

Jacklyn, not affected by her grandmother's hopelessness, continued her icy tone,

"Don't be so dramatic grandma. BoysTown is helping.
I'm listening, doing what I am supposed to do, and I shower and wash my hair EVERYDAY!"

Fran turned her body towards Jacklyn and asked,

"Really? You're lying! Your hair tells a different story.
You're not even complying with the basic hygiene regimen."

"ARGH! When are you ever going to listen and trust me?!"

I realized that neither Jacklyn nor Fran was going to give, and

I caught a glimpse of sincerity in Jacklyn's expressions and words, I intervened.

> "Fran, let's try something. I want you to hold your tongue for a few minutes and let's explore what Jacklyn is telling us. Can you do that?"
>
> "I'll try."
>
> "Thank you. Okay, Jacklyn, please walk us through your shower routine."

Jacklyn sighed,

> "What? So, the two of you can team up on me and tell me I'm doing everything wrong?!"
>
> "No, not at all. I want to understand your process and explore if there's an easy and simple explanation for the state of your hair."
>
> "OK. FINE! After dinner and chores, it's my turn to shower. I go into the bathroom. I start the water. I take off my clothes and get in. Is this really necessary, Andrea?!"
>
> "I think it will help. Bear with me and my annoying questions for a few minutes."
>
> "Where was I? That's right, I get in the shower. I wash my body."

I interrupted with a clarifying question,

> "Do you use a bar of soap or liquid soap?"
>
> "Bar."
>
> "Okay. Please continue."
>
> "I put some shampoo in my hands and lather. I then massage it in my hair. I rinse it out. I then take some conditioner and put

that throughout my hair."

"How much conditioner do you use?"

"I DON'T KNOW."

I shot her my stern therapist face and said,

"Can you show me? This part is really important."

She complied and showed a dab of conditioner in the palm of her hand.

"How long do you rinse your hair after you put the conditioner in your hair?"

"Until I no longer feel the conditioner."

"Hmmm...so it's not the amount of conditioner or your rinse out. It sounds like you are doing a great job washing your body, shampooing, and conditioning. Okay, what happens after you condition?"

"I stay under the hot water for a little bit longer and then turn off the water. I grab my towel, wrap it around my body, and then get out of the shower. I wrap my hair with another towel. I grab my pajamas and put them on. That's it."

"Okay, thank you. What do you do after you put pajamas on?"

"I grab my brush and take it to Larissa. Larissa puts product in my hair and combs it out."

A light bulb went off.

"What product does Larissa use?"

"I don't know. The one she uses on her hair."

"AH!" I sat back and allowed the easy and simple explanation to form in my mind. Jacklyn and Fran stared at me and waited for me to stop carrying on and explain myself.

I looked at Fran and explained,

"Larissa's Black."

"I know that. What does that have to do with how greasy Jacklyn's hair is?"

Then it hit me—the various required hair care practices of different races is not common knowledge. Fran was born in rural America and had little exposure and few interactions with Black women and didn't know this.

I leaned in and explained.

"White people hair is not the same as Black people hair. The two types of hair require different processes and products. Larissa put oil on Jacklyn's hair because that is how she cares for her own hair. She didn't know that Jacklyn's hair would become greasy. So, you see, Fran, Jacklyn is showering and washing her hair every day. Her greasy hair is due to the oil Larissa is treating it with."

The light bulbs went off for Jacklyn and Fran.

"See! Grandma! I'm getting better, you just wouldn't listen!"

As adults, the authority figure, especially when we are used to power struggles and oppositional behavior, we can get stuck in thinking we're right and desperately wanting our child to listen without question. But sometimes, we're the ones who need to listen to what they're saying. Hold our tongues like

Fran did in this story and get to the bottom of the issue.

How do we do this?

We sit back and fight against our natural inclination to think we know and understand what is going on. Because sometimes, a lot of the time, we don't have all the answers (and that's okay). And a lot of the time we jump to conclusions.

So, we need to take a breath (or a few) and go at it from a position of wanting to learn. Put on your Dora the Explorer cap and engage in active listening.

Here are the steps for active listening:

Eliminate all distractions. This means both you and your child should have all your attention on the conversation. All screens are put away and not accessible. I know this is a lot to ask of both of you, but trust me, it's necessary. Let me show you.

Think about a time when you wanted to share an intense emotion you were experiencing with your partner and they were looking at their phone the whole time and occasionally saying, "Yeah. Oh. Ah ha."

Did you feel loved at that moment? Did you feel heard?

Probably not, so let's start with this step. Set up a time where all distractions can be laid to rest, and you'll have some uninterrupted time.

Look at your child. Ideally, y'all would be looking at each other. However, when it comes to kids sharing vulnerable stuff, it's sometimes easier for them if the eye contact suggestion of active listening is removed.

Eye contact in these situations may make them uncomfortable, and if they're already experiencing uncomfy feelings from being vulnerable, we don't want to lay it on too thick.

A guest on my podcast, Sara Hegarty, tends to have these conversations while driving with her children. She has found that not looking at each other works for them. That's acceptable if it's mutually agreed upon.

But you, as the listener, should look at them unless they ask you not to. Again, this is a way for them to feel like you're listening to them. Remember the goal is for them to share their feelings, not check off all the active listening skills checkboxes. Figure out what works for y'all and run with it.

Reflect what your child is saying. For this step, channel a mirror. When they state they're experiencing a feeling, you say something to the effect of, "It seems like you're (insert feeling)."

My other tip in this step is to lead with empathy. Say things like, "That is awful." "That must have been hard."

Do you struggle with empathy and hence don't know what to say?

I get it, many of my clients do, too. Take a moment. Ask yourself, "What emotion would I be feeling in this situation?" Think of a time you have felt that emotion and channel that. Then enter that feeling into that phrase.

Seek additional information. This may be the most challenging of the steps because of our natural tendency to ask, "Why?" "Why" puts people on the defensive. We don't want them to be on guard. We want them to feel like they're being heard. Use language that is exploratory in nature. For example, use open-ended questions that keep conversations going.

Refrain from asking closed-ended questions (think yes-no questions) because that limits where the conversation can go.

Here are some great ways to get additional information:

 Tell me about...

 How did you...

 In what ways...

 What's it like...

Active listening is not easy, but it's a skill, which means you can get better at it...the more you practice. It needs to become a habit. This becomes even more difficult when emotions are high, so practice when emotions are not high.

Let's recap the four active listening steps:

 Eliminate all distractions

 Look at your child.

 Reflect what your child is saying.

 Seek additional information

Active listening requires you to focus, look, reflect, and ask. It's a foundational skill that can improve all relationships.

I continued to work with Fran and Jacklyn for the rest of my internship year at BoysTown. Fran's active listening skills improved leaps and bounds and Jacklyn blossomed within all the structure BoysTown provided her—something she never experienced before.

This was not Fran's fault. Fran was Jacklyn's grandmother who had been tasked with raising another child, all alone, when she was in her 60's because Jacklyn's parents wouldn't choose Jacklyn over drugs.

As I departed BoysTown, our conversations focused on which place—Fran's home or staying at BoysTown—would give Jacklyn the best chance for a successful life.

And unfortunately reader, I leave you in suspense, because I myself don't know.

I like to believe Jacklyn stayed at BoysTown, continued to strengthen her relationship with Fran, developed both the coping skills and life skills she needed, graduated high school, stayed away from drugs and alcohol that didn't serve her parents well, went to culinary school, opened her own bakery, and is slated to be on the next season of The Great American Baking Show.

QUALITY OVER QUANTITY

"I don't want them to go to school because then I won't see them enough."

Autumn, a mother of four children ranging in ages from 2 to 8 years, expressed to me.

"Talk to me about whether homeschooling is working for you and your family at this time," I replied.

Autumn paused, looked at her husband, shrugged her shoulders, looked down, and wept.

I motioned for Corey to hand her a tissue. Corey scootched towards Autumn, wrapped his arm around her, and squeezed. We sat in silence for a few moments, giving Autumn time to feel her feels. When she was ready to continue the conversation, she'd let us know. Autumn took a deep breath and made eye contact.

"I want it to work. I want an old-fashioned lifestyle for my family."

"Believe me, I get that. Talk to me about your vision for this old-fashioned lifestyle."

"The kids would be home with me all day. I would homeschool them with little problems and they would enjoy it. Corey would work from home, and he would come and hangout for work breaks. We would all feel connected."

"But Honey, Ethan is like me," Corey interjected. "He needs more structure. And organization and structure are not some of your strengths."

"But they could be."

I took a breath and in my warmest clinical psychologist voice, asked,

"At what cost to you, Autumn? I don't know about you, but I'm not willing to sacrifice your well-being for this old-fashioned lifestyle that may not be the best fit for each of your kids."

Autumn heard this and the tissue immediately went back and caught the tears. Corey squeezed her shoulders and positioned his face to make eye contact.

"I second what Andrea said. I'm not willing to sacrifice your well-being."

Autumn and Corey embraced, and I gave them a few moments to experience this tender moment before I continued.

"Autumn, I hear you want a loving and connected family. I want that for you too. Please explain how sending the kids to school prevents a loving and connected family?"

"Because they will be gone from nine in the morning until three in the afternoon, and then if they do extracurriculars, that will be less time together. I want them with me as much as possible. How could we connect with so little time?"

"Because you focus on quality over quantity when it comes to time. I would much rather send my children to school and not feel stressed out and overwhelmed so that when they are at home with me and my husband that they have two completely present parents who want nothing more than to spend time with them — connecting. Our children need quality time, they don't need ALL the time."

"Maybe it's time for me to find some friends who don't homeschool their children."

"BAA HAA HA! You may be on to something."

Too often we get caught up and focus on the number of hours we are spending with our children. I blame our society's obsession with the 40-hour work week or punching the clock and getting paid by the hour instead of by the task*.

Let's not allow this ineffective practice to invade our family life. Connecting with your children and forming an attachment is less about the amount of time and much more about the quality of the time together. A stronger attachment can be formed in 15 minutes of quality time compared to 60 minutes of being in the same room together.

And given that busyness is the new status symbol in America, we focus on the amount of time we do things instead of the quality of the time together. This focus leads us to erroneously think others will think we are a great parent if we say, "Oh yeah, I spent an hour with my children today" compared to if we say, "Oh, yeah, I spent 15 minutes with my children today." The first one sounds "better."

But that is fake parenting bullshit that I don't want any of you engaging in. It is toxic!

When you're in a group of parents and one parent is flaunting how much they do for their child or how much time they spend

---

*Why can't we live in a more task-oriented society? You know, where the boss tells you what they expect from you today and once you accomplish that task, well then you get to go home. Damn government jobs!

with their child, I would like you to ask yourself (not them, we don't want to burst their fake bubble),

"Yeah, but how much of that is actually quality time where you're connecting with your child?"

I bet that question will stop your automatic thoughts—where you are comparing yourself to this other parent and "losing"—dead in its tracks. Because you're reading this book and implementing parenting tips that work and therefore, you're "WINNING!"

How do we do this?

 Become aware of the brief moments when you're with your child, when you can stop what you're doing and connect with them. It doesn't even need to be minutes. It can literally be seconds:
>Give your child a hug
>Mess with their hair
>Yell "HEY, ETHAN! YOU'RE ADORED!"

 When they want to show you something, get into a good place of what you're doing (use the finger signal* as needed), get down to their level, and then spend the amount of time they deem necessary to allow them to show you what they want to show you. Use open ended statements like, "Tell me about your _____."

---

*Hold up your pointer finger, indicating that you need them to be quiet and patient for a minute. Keep your pointer finger up until you are ready to give your child your undivided attention.

How many times have you assumed what their drawing is and got it wrong? And then their feelings are hurt, and the quality time is ruined! YIKES!

When it comes to time with your child, remember it's less about how much and more about how good.

The homeschooling vs. hybrid schooling vs. private schooling is an ongoing debate in therapy for Autumn and Corey, and when I say Autumn AND Corey, you all know I really just mean Autumn, right?!

But hey! Autumn is a "Meghan" and that's who I'm truly writing this book for. So, I'll continue to work with Autumn and help her decide what type of schooling is in the best interest of each of her children AND her well-being.

LET THEM LEAD

Charlotte, 6-year-old girl, Andrea (mother), Jim (father)

"*NAILED IT!*"

Charlotte screamed after she noticed the flying disc landed within 20 feet of where Andrea was standing.

Andrea smiled and laughed at her daughter's excitement, and reinforced her daughter's enthusiasm with

"*Great work, Baby Girl!*"

Five minutes into their playing catch with the flying disc, Jim walked over and stood by Andrea.

"*NAILED IT!*"

Jim waited a whopping two throws before he provided his peanut gallery comment.

"*Baby Girl, to 'nail' a throw, it should go directly to Mama. Maybe she takes one step in any direction, but that's it. Making Mama run 15 feet is not a 'NAILED IT' throw.*"

Charlotte's body language deflated and all her exuberance dissipated.

Seeing this, Andrea "angry eyed" Jim. And purposely threw the flying disc 30 feet from Charlotte and screamed, "*NAILED IT!*" She then shot Jim a "I dare you to say something look."

Charlotte chased it, fell in the process, and the mother daughter pair laughed and laughed.

GAME ON!

"NAILED IT!"

Alex, 6-year-old boy, Jesse (father)

"Daddy, will you play dinosaurs with me?"

Jesse's internal monologue: "NOT DINOSAURS! ANYTHING BUT DINOSAURS! No respectable paleontologist allows their child to believe that the Brachiosaurus, Stegosaurus, Tyrannosaurus Rex, and Triceratops were all alive during the same period."

"Sure, Alex. BUT only if we specify the period. We can play with dinosaurs during the Jurassic Period—such as the Brachiosaurus and Stegosaurus—or the Cretaceous Period, with Triceratops and Tyrannosaurs Rex. But absolutely no mixing."

"But Daddy, my T-Rex and Brachiosaurus are best friends! Why can't they play together?"

Jesse perked up and went into lecture mode.

"Because they would have never been..."

Alex recognized the shift, grabbed his dinosaurs, and went to another room to play.

Christine, 36-year-old, Andrea (clinical child psychologist)

"Okay, Christine, the Lord knows you have your hands full with four children and Edward isn't helpful, what with him leaving the house at 5:00am and not returning until 7:00pm. You've got a lot on your plate: homeschooling, grocery shopping, cooking, keeping everyone alive, cleaning—all while your OCD is wreaking havoc. So, we want to focus on quality time over quantity of time with each child."

Christine looked at me despairingly and stated,

"I don't know what quality time with my kids looks like."

"What do you and the kids like to do for fun?"

Christine shrugged her shoulders and cried.

Whew! I still get choked up when I think about that session with Christine. When I realized there are parents out there that struggle to engage in child-centered play, and my husband is one of them, it broke my heart.

But I'm a firm believer in the saying, "People don't know what they don't know." So first let's start with what exactly is child-centered play. It's when we allow our child to dictate what and how we play. It could be imaginary play where there are no established rules, and you make up a story as you go. Or it can be a board game with well-established rules, but you allow your child creative freedom so they may alter and change the rules as they see fit.

Some may immediately think this is some foo-foo new age way of parenting their child that leads their child to become a free spirit that rejects structure and goes against the man. But please remember who is writing this book. My first and foremost goal for writing this book was, and still is, to help parents raise children who will not be 35 and living in their basement. I'm not advocating child-centered play all the time, just some of it. And here's why:

I find engaging in child-centered play relaxing and less demanding. The rules may change, but I'm not the one having to change them. It very well may look like the card game scene from *Big Daddy*—where the kid keeps changing the rules.

But roll with it! I just go along with what they say, only occasionally purposely messing with them by violating their rules (I am oppositional after all) and enjoy the freedom that comes with someone else being in charge.

If you're like me, a lot of my time is spent leading others. Engaging in child-centered play gives me the opportunity to follow instead of lead. It takes the pressure off me and allows my children to develop leadership skills and creativity. Many parents want to raise the future leaders of America, but they don't provide them the time and space to develop the skills. Child-centered play allows them to develop and practice leadership skills.

They can practice autonomy, decision making, and creativity skills. They decide the plot lines, the rules, and how people should interact with others. They can test out different interpersonal skills and see which ones are effective in getting others to engage in their play with them. It turns out that strong-arming people into what you want them to do is probably not the best way to lead others.

But I get it. It's challenging for some parents (Cough, cough, cough. Jim, Jesse, Christine) to relinquish control and let their children take the reins.

Here are some tips to thriving in child-centered play:

 Put away all your distractions. This means your cell phone, computer, tablet, newspaper, or book. Be completely present with your children.

 Tell your child they get to choose what you all will do and how you will do it. Remind yourself that you're training them to be a future leader of America.

Refrain from all criticism. I mean, what's the likelihood they're going to burn down the house? And only provide suggestions if they specifically ask you for them.

 Find the joy. You may not want to play that. You may not even like it. It may even grind your gears, but focus on what you value: your connection with your child. Their smile. Their laugh. Them being assertive. Bask in that.

 Use shaping* on yourself. Set a timer for child-centered play to 5 minutes. Then increase the time as you get better at it.

Don't be a Jim, Jesse, or Christine.

Be an Andrea.

Our son Connor was given the "Future President" award by his kindergarten teacher for his leadership skills...see what child-centered play can do for your child.

*Remember the "Treat Your Child's Behavior Like Play-Doh" parenting tip?

ROUGHHOUSING

"How has the week been?" I asked Betty and Archie, parents to a three-year-old boy, Forsythe, who was about to get kicked out of his in-home daycare because he's aggressive towards other kids. He's known as the kid who cusses, hits, bites, and throws toys at others—the kid that everyone wants to be friends with.

The daycare provider, Mrs. Thornton is a wonderfully patient woman, but she's concerned that the parents of the other kids will start complaining and pull their children out of her home.

"It was awful, Andrea."

"What does awful look like, Betty?"

"Well, we were outside with Forsythe playing, and the two neighbor kids came over. The three of them were playing nicely, but then, ARGH, Forsythe threw grass at one of the neighbor kids."

"Grass?"

"Yeah, he tore some off from the lawn and threw it at the smaller of the two neighbor kids."

"Umm...was this lead filled, poisonous, grass?"

Archie laughed. Betty side-eyed me.

I put my hands up, signaling no more sarcasm.

"Okay, okay, in all seriousness, we know Forsythe is ALL boy, right?"

"Right!" Betty and Archie said in unison.

"Given that he is ALL boy, in what ways is he allowed to channel his aggression in a socially appropriate way?"

Crickets! Both of their eyes shot to the ceiling.

Awkward!

"Okay. How often do y'all roughhouse with Forsythe?"

Archie shot Betty a look. You know the one I'm talking about, where the head slightly tilts to one side and forward, one eyebrow raises, and the lips pucker every so faintly.

Betty looked at the ceiling again.

Archie then looked at me, using a defeated tone, and said,

"Never."

Betty's eyes stopped looking at the ceiling and met mine.

"Well, we thought roughhousing would make him more aggressive, and the Lord knows, we don't need him to be MORE aggressive."

"Well, actually, roughhousing has gotten a really bad rep over the last few years, but it's a great way to socially appropriately channel aggression. And research shows that it neither makes children aggressive, nor does it make aggressive children more aggressive. It has a lot of benefits, such as...*"

Archie interrupted,

"Wait! So, you're telling me, if I roughhouse with Forsythe, he'll probably be less aggressive with other kids?"

---

*...becoming aware of their own needs, learning to speak up, reading others' emotions, respecting others' boundaries, regulating their reactive behaviors, and navigating conflict.

"Yep."

Both their mouths dropped!

"And he probably wouldn't get kicked out of day care?"

"Probably not, but no promises."

"Shit! I'll go get him right now and rough him up!"

Archie said, as he pretended to stand up and leave.

Fast forward one week, I was in another session with Betty and Archie, and I asked them how roughhousing with Forsythe went.

"OH MY GOODNESS, Andrea! It was hilarious! Archie started approaching Forsythe in a playful way, all while saying, 'I'm going to rough you up, boy!' Forsythe had no idea what to do. He turned, ran, hid behind me, all while screaming."

Archie, very proud of himself, chimed in with,

"I crouched down as if I was a wrestler, leaped towards him, grabbed him, threw him over my shoulder, carried him to the carpet, threw him down, and started pushing and tugging at him. It took him a little bit to figure out what was going on, but then, Andrea, you should have seen him. He had a huge smile on his face, and he was eventually running and launching himself at me. He now asks to roughhouse every night."

"And Betty, how was it watching Archie and Forsythe rough-house?"

"Well, you know, at first I was super nervous, I grew the boy in my own body for ten months!

> But once Forsythe got into it...OH MY GOODNESS! It was adorable and I'm here for it."

"And how many negative reports from Mrs. Thornton has Forsythe earned?"

Their eyes met. Betty, with a tinge of embarrassment said,

> "Ever since Archie started roughhousing with him... Forsythe hasn't been aggressive towards the other kids..."

I smiled my self-righteous smile and said, "You don't say..."

The three of us laughed.

> "I'm so proud of the...wait, Betty have you roughhoused with Forsythe?"

Betty sheepishly said, "No."

> "What's preventing you from roughhousing with your son?"

Betty paused and then replied,

> "I don't know how—my parents never roughhoused with me."

"Would you be willing to try?"

With some hesitation, Betty said, "Yes."

And that was the only response I needed before I kicked down the damn door and told her how to roughhouse.

I can never preach enough the impact parents roughhousing with their child has on their relationship and the child's behavior.

How do I know roughhousing is good above and beyond the research findings I shared with Betty and Archie? Because unlike Betty, roughhousing with both my father and three older brothers was common for me growing up. I would not back down, and seeing that three out of four of them were over six feet tall, and all of them weighed over 200lbs, it was a David and Goliath type of situation.

Roughhousing is something my husband and I do with our children, and we've never (knock on wood) received word that our children violate others' boundaries.

They love it!

I tell my kids, "I'm gonna rough you up!" They respond with, "Bring it, Mama!"

Goodness! Just hearing them say that, warms my heart!

If you're like me and already roughhouse with your child, here's your gold star. But maybe you're like Betty and don't know what roughhousing looks like but are willing to try. If that's the case, here's what I told Betty:

 Establish a designated space. Think any carpet. No need to get bougie and spend money. We're going for practical here. Push the furniture to the side, leaving cushioned ottomans if your child is an American Ninja Warrior in training. And clear the space of any sharp objects.

 Channel baby chimpanzees or other primates. Pull. Tug. Wrap arms and legs around them. Put part of your body weight on them—we aren't going for suffocation here. Push. Slap (again, gently!) We aren't crossing the line into abuse.

Give immediate feedback. If anyone during roughhousing feels pain, they should say so. This way, the other person learns their behaviors have consequences. Then the person can adjust their behavior in real time.

 Voice boundaries. Say when you don't like something. For example, I'm claustrophobic, and don't tolerate not being able to move. So, if this happens during roughhousing, I will immediately let the others know I don't like that. This helps others know what your boundaries are AND provides them with an opportunity to practice respecting boundaries.

 Monitor emotions. If anyone experiences frustration or anger pops up, they're expected to regulate their emotions. Deep breaths or other grounding techniques—stay tuned for "The No. 2 Parenting Book: Coping Skills" edition. Take a quick break. Let emotions come down and then try again.

 At the end: check in, show positive affection. When most members have deemed that the roughhousing session is over, then check in with everyone. Make sure everyone is good. And hug it out!

Now, go channel your inner monkey, and wrestle.

I'm not 100% sure what happened with Archie, Betty, and Forsythe, but I'm confident they're doing okay and Forsythe is not on the verge of getting expelled from school for his aggressive behaviors like throwing grass at other children. I would've heard about it from "the streets."

FEEL THE PARENTING BURN

"Maybe, just maybe, I'll get sick and then...I can have a few days break. I wouldn't have to work. I could get some additional help from Jim or my parents. I'd get a little break from being a mom. I could wrap myself up in my peacock blanket, lay in bed, eat chicken noodle soup, and watch mindless TV.

"YES! Housewives of New Jersey started a few weeks ago, I could watch all those episodes. Oh, that would be great.

"WAIT!

"As long as I got sick on a Friday or Saturday. Or else that would be way too much maneuvering of the schedule. That'd cause more hassle than simply continuing to do everything.

"Now, if only I could make that happen..."

If you EVER find yourself trying to manifest a sickness because that's an easy way to get some help and hence a break from parenting, then you might be experiencing parental burnout. Parental burnout is when your responsibilities as a parent significantly outweigh your resources.

The signs of parental burnout include:

- ☐ Thinking, "I just can't" when you're thinking about what you must do with or for your kid
- ☐ Not getting anything done
- ☐ Taking much longer than usual to complete tasks
- ☐ Not being excited to do things with your children

If you marked any of these four, I know what you're thinking.

NO, you're not a terrible parent.

Yes, we all love being parents (or else you wouldn't be reading a parenting book), but if we're being honest, it can also be life-sucking and frustrating as hell.

AND it's not like there are two weeks of paid vacation from being a parent per year.

Parental burnout is real!

Psychologists estimate that 5.5 million American parents experience clinically significant levels of parental burnout.

5.5 million!

That's the population of Chicago, San Diego, and Dallas all together.

Some of you might be thinking, "So what?! Andrea. Parenting is challenging. DUH!"

The reason every parent should try to prevent burnout* is when we're burned out, our autopilot activates and we're simply going through the motions. We detach from our child. All that work you put in building a high-quality relationship with your child goes down the toilet. We stop making daily deposits into our child, throw off our ratio, and we're simply trying to survive.

This is the last parenting pointer in this book.

---

*Remember during the Taming Temper Tantrums tip, I talked about the best way to treat tantrums is to prevent them? Same goes for parental burnout. If parental burnout goes unchecked, then parents throw their own tantrums.

You should know by now that I don't want you and your child to be merely surviving.

I want y'all thriving!

A great way I've found to ward off parental burnout is a parentcation. A parentcation is when you get a short period of time, I typically advocate for 48 hours*, where you have absolutely no responsibilities and you spend the 48 hours doing anything and everything YOU want to do.

I've recommended both momcations and dadcations to my clients countless times.

I take a momcation each year, and let me tell you, they're absolutely amazing!

Jim takes the kids on a Friday evening, around 5:00pm, to our place on the lake. I then get to decide what I'm going to eat for dinner, breakfast, lunch, dinner, breakfast, and another lunch.

Can you imagine that?

Only having to fix one meal. Eating your food when it's warm. Eating what your body tells you it wants. No one leaning or hanging on you as you eat.

Wait for it...eating a meal from start to finish WITHOUT being interrupted!

GASP!

You may be thinking, "Andrea! That can actually happen? Where do I sign up for such a thing?"

WAIT! There's more! (Think infomercial)

---

*It can also be as short as you got, but I'd say at least 24 hours, if you can. 48 hours is my gold standard!

Then, there's sleeping and napping however many hours you want. You can go to bed when you want. Wake up when you want. Nap if you want. SLEEP! Glorious, glorious sleep!

And finally, there's doing whatever you want. I typically go for a long bike ride one day and then a long hike the next.

During one of my momcations, I organized and cleaned up toys, not because I had to or was required to, but because I legitimately wanted to. Now please don't get it twisted. Do NOT fill the time with work or catching up on "have tos" unless you genuinely receive pleasure from the activity.

Now... I may have watched a full season of the Netflix show *Dead to Me* as I organized and cleaned, but that's because it was my momcation, darn it!

Now, before you start thinking that I am a heartless jerk*, I do give Jim dadcations.

His typically come in the form of going to the lake with one or both of his best friends for a guy's weekend. No children! Lots and lots of adult beverages are consumed. A round of golf is typically played. You know, bro stuff.

Parentcations truly are wonderful, and I'm a huge advocate for people taking at least one a year.

And if you're sitting there thinking, "Who really has time for all that?"

I'd argue, given the negative consequences associated with parental burnout, that you can't afford not to.

---

*Hopefully, you don't already think that by this point, and if you did, you probably stopped reading by now!

So, if you find yourself in a burned-out state, it's time to take a parentcation! Remember, we want to try to prevent burnout, so track how often you get burned out and plan parentcations appropriately.

For me, I could probably use a second momcation each year, but that doesn't work for the season my family is in. Keeping the whole premise of this book in mind—practicality—find what works for you and yours.

The biggest barrier you will most likely face to taking a parentcation is fighting against our society's view that they're a sign of weakness or that you aren't a good enough parent. Parentcations are neither of those things. Tell the person (or yourself) to shut up! With that said, we're going to need to get vulnerable and ask the people in our lives for a parentcation.

Steps for asking for a parentcation:

 Recognize and acknowledge you need a parentcation

 Schedule a time to chat (seems far less ominous than "can we talk") with your partner or other folks you'd trust with your children

 Take a deep breath

 Attend scheduled chatting time

 Explain that you're experiencing parental burnout

 Ask for 48 hours where all your responsibilities can be removed

 Show your appreciation (assuming they say yes)

Figure out logistics (i.e., dates—during the week or weekend, will you be going or will everyone else be going, what's the budget)

 When the day comes, be ready for the guilt. It will try to convince you that you aren't really burned out and that you can handle it. And that you don't really need this silly thing called a momcation.

LIES! Please know these are all lies. Acknowledge the guilt and take your parentcation anyway.

 Enjoy!

BONUS for Single Parents:

I get it. You don't have a partner to take the kids off your hands, but that doesn't mean that you don't deserve a parentcation. You may be more deserving than the rest of us.

My first and foremost suggestion would be to ask your family, again folks who you trust with taking your children for 48 hours. If that isn't an option, let me introduce you to what I like to call the Parentcation Exchange Program.

 Find another single parent who you would trust with your child(ren) and you don't find theirs annoying as hell

 Chat with them about parental burnout and ask them if they would like to enter into a parentcation exchange program with you. They take your child(ren) for 48 hours so that you get your parentcation and then you take their child(ren) for 48 hours so that

they can have a parentcation. Each single parent gets their parentcation and the kids get to play!

It's a win-win for everybody.

My momcation looked a little bit different this year and I may be in need of another—especially after *finally* publishing this book.

My momcation was spent driving two hours, checking in for a sprint triathlon, meeting with a neurologist, clinical psychologist, and a geneticist and learning all about Huntington's Disease for three hours, checking into a hotel, learning that one of my senior high school football players completely shattered his right leg—ending his football career, talking with our first year coach and his position coach because he was struggling with how this could happen to a senior who has done everything we've asked him to do, eating too spicy chicken tikka masala, binge watching the second half of the second season of *Lincoln Lawyer*, and that was just Friday.

Saturday, I woke up at 4:00am, swam 700m, biked 13 miles (mostly uphill—bastards!), ran a 5k, ate an overstuffed sandwich, drank a swinging hammock, went back to the hotel, showered, left the hotel (I ain't paying $330/night!), drove two hours home, and binge watched Quarterbacks on Netflix.

Woke up on Sunday morning with all the intention of lying on the couch and doing absolutely nothing until Jim and the kids got home around 3:00pm.

Yeah that didn't happen.

My mom called me in the morning. She fell in the bathroom, the ambulance was on their way to transport her to the ER. She broke three bones in her foot and I spent the rest of my momcation helping her and my dad. See, no one wants that momcation.

BUT it was a momcation nonetheless. And you better believe, I look forward to my next one.

ACT LIKE YOU'RE A GREAT PARENT

You can do it*!

Parenting is tough, but you have what it takes to take your metaphorical bull by the horns and be less pooped out.

Being "pooped out" is a feeling. Directly changing your feelings is impossible–you might as well try to go a day without scraping toothpaste off a wall, sink or out of someone's hair.

Challenging your thoughts and developing new, more helpful thinking patterns takes time and ain't nobody got time for that. You're too busy shuttling your child from hockey to school to Mandarin tutoring to their skate time.

But changing your behaviors, doing something different, simply takes a commitment to try something new because what you've been doing isn't working for you and yours.

That's where one of my favorite sayings, "Fake It Until You Make It," comes into play.

In those pooped out parenting moments, when you just can't anymore, you're at your wits end and your homeostasis is out of whack, remember what your goal is: to parent your children in a way that centers around high expectations within the context of the warm and fuzzies.

And choose to act like you're a great parent.

Choose joy. See the joy in your children and remember why you chose to have children in the first place. (Everyone chooses to be a parent. You all know how babies are made.

---

*Say this phrase just like Rob Schneider in Adam Sandler's *Waterboy*

Therefore, you engaged in actions that would get you this bundle of joy, now commit to engaging in actions that lead them towards your goal.)

Lots of people falsely perceive me as a "perfect parent." But let me let you in on a teenie tiny secret–I'm not. Not even close.

I have days where I'm screaming inside and I just can't take the incredible loudness that comes with having two 7 year olds and a 5 year old. And there are times when I don't act in alignment with my "act like you're a great parent" call to action and I raise my voice and yell out of frustration or stress (usually when I'm trying to get the kids out the door for school and myself to an early TV appearance or a talk that day), but then I thank God I have lots of positives banked, I apologize.

And I use the 3 R's of recovering from a mistake.

 Recognize: you just made a mistake and that's okay

 Regroup: practice 5-2-8 breathing

 Refocus: what's one parenting tip from this book that you can act on and just do it (I'll take any sponsorships from Nike)

You get to choose whether you're going to continue to be a pooped out parent. You can practice the tips in this book or not. The choice is yours.

And as the Grail Knight in *Indiana Jones and the Last Crusade* said, "But choose wisely, for while the true Grail will bring you life, the false Grail will take it from you."

Similarly, choose parenting practices that bring you and yours life and leave the others behind.

ACKNOWLEDGEMENTS

I don't have words. I used them all up writing this book.

AND because there aren't enough words that adequately describe the impact the folks listed on this page had on me writing my first book. But nonetheless, they deserve at least a sentence or two in an attempt.

Jim Hubbell: My best friend, husband, and co-parent (not an easy gig when you're married to someone who literally wrote a book on parenting). Reader, you have him to thank (or write nasty emails to) for the book you just read.

Nikki Diederich: My editor and friend. I hope this process has been more enjoyable than reading and grading undergraduate papers.

Lauren Marshall: My graphic designer, customer avatar, and female best friend (you can only have one best friend). Maybe this book will sell a million copies (manifestation) and I can finally hire you to be the "Senior Creative Director" at BrightSpot Families.

Adam Lauritsen: My illustrator and friend. I'm in awe of your ability to take my random descriptions and make them adorable and humorous.

Anne Beekman: My page layout guru. Where were you when I needed my 200-page dissertation formatted?!

Dave Essinger and his Creative Writing Class: My workshoppers. I appreciate Dave's suggestion of starting in the stories. The students' desires for more of the book gave me hope that others might actually want to read it.

Eva Daniel: My beta reader and humor stick. Let's remember, I'm funny for a clinical psychologist, not a comedian.

Brian Jewel: The kicker of my arse. You telling me "I want your book in my hands" was the turning point. Had you not said this to me, I would've continued getting distracted by one of my other bajillion ideas, and never fulfilled a dream of being an author.

Adriana Mata and Emily Browning: More of my beta readers. Your reassurance that my sarcasm landed and didn't make me come off like a huge bitch was helpful.

The Avengers: My cheerleaders, supporters, and shit caller outers. These entrepreneurs have a wealth of information they willingly share, but watch out, they will be brutally honest and tell you when you're making excuses.

Dale Dustin: My book mentor and friend. How often do you regret sending that LinkedIn message?

Fidel and Carolyn: My parents. Your parenting practices of parenting using high expectations within the context of the warm and fuzzies was the guiding principle for this book. I couldn't have dreamed up better parents, but don't get it twisted, I still know way more about parenting than the two of you.

Fidel Mata: My oldest brother. You wrote in *The Day the Babies Crawled Away* that there is no such thing as a parenting manual. Well...maybe there is now, and your "lil nerd" wrote it.

Charlotte, Connor, and Chloe Hubbell: My children and guinea pigs. You three bring joy, laughter, and a lot of noise to my life (thank goodness for Loop noise reducing ear plugs), and gave me great stories for this book."

Made in the USA
Las Vegas, NV
29 December 2023